Lilith: Adam's First Wife
and
Other Dramatic Readings

by

Meg Bowman

* **Lilith: Adam's First Wife**

* **George Sand:
  Deviant Extraordinaire**

* **Harriet Ross Tubman:
  Dramatic Reading**

* **Feelings**

* **Moon Goddess**

* **Circle of Sisterhood**

Dramatic Readings on Feminist Issues, Vol. IV

ISBN 0-940483-13-0

c. 1996

HOT FLASH PRESS
P.O. Box 21506,
San Jose, CA 95151
(408) 292-1172

Other books available from Hot Flash Press:

FEMINIST CLASSICS: WOMEN'S WORDS THAT CHANGED
THE WORLD   *(a reader)* $7.95

READINGS FOR WOMEN'S PROGRAMS *(expanded)* $ 8.95

MEMORIAL SERVICES FOR WOMEN $8.95

READINGS FOR OLDER WOMEN $11.95

GODDESSES, WITCHES & THE PARADIGM SHIFT $14.95

WOMEN'S HISTORY: DRAMATIC READINGS $12.95
*(Sappho; Hypatia; Mary Wollstonecraft; Deborah Sampson; Emma Goldman;
Elizabeth Gurley Flynn)*

DRAMATIC READINGS ON FEMINIST ISSUES $10.95

Spiral Bound:

Greek Goddesses Rising	$5.95
FUN FLYERS	$6.95
GROSS FLYERS	$6.95
SILLY FLYERS	$8.95
OFFICE TALES: DON'T PUSH IT	$9.95
NICE FLYERS	$9.95

AUTHOR
Meg Bowman teaches sociology at San Jose State University *(northern
California)*. An ardent feminist, Meg is active in NOW, OWL, and the
Women & Religion Task Force *(Unitarian Universalist Association)*. Meg
is co-chair of the Feminist Caucus, American Humanist Association,
and she designs, organizes and escorts international study tours; she also
collects contributions to sponsor impoverished young Kenyan and Ro-
manian women through school.

LILITH: ADAM'S FIRST WIFE

and
Other Dramatic Readings

* **Lilith: Adam's First Wife**

* **George Sand: Deviant Extraordinaire**

* **Harriet Ross Tubman: Dramatic Reading**

* **Feelings**

* **Moon Goddess**

* **Circle of Sisterhood**

EDUCATIONAL AND FUN

No Memorizing

Use in the classroom; as Women's History Month programs; NOW, NWPC, LWV, AAUW, UUWF, Girl Scout, or union meetings; religious programs, and for Women's Retreats.

Dedication:

For my two
granddaughters,
Christine Ann
and
Lindsey Rhiannon.

May they continue
to challenge patriarchy,
the oldest
of injustices.

**Special thanks to Jean Shiota for her
"magical" computer skills.**

To be yourself in a world which is doing its best to make you just like everybody else means to fight the greatest battle there is or ever will be.

e.e. cummings

With wisdom,

knowing our past,

we help shape the future.

READ BETWEEN THE LINES

Because I'm a woman I lack something
in history. I've learned of the lands Kings gained
through the glorious end of soldiers' lives,
and how courtly were King Arthur's knights.

And I've read Dante's poems for Beatrice,
and I've read Shakespeare's contemplations
on death.
I've learned how Man emerged from
a primordial stew,
and how from Man the Hunter society grew.

Yet despite all this knowledge there's something
I'm lacking.
According to His-tory, all women were passive.
Women were silent dolls in courtly games,
and when they had brains they used men's names
for pen names.

Women's true history has been repressed,
So I'll search for my heritage in His-tory's silences.

> —Anonymous
> *(who was a woman)*

Historical sociologists study the past to better understand the present and, hopefully, change the future.

LILITH: ADAM'S FIRST WIFE
and Other Dramatic Readings

by
Meg Bowman

TABLE OF CONTENTS

Responsive Readings:

<u>Dramatic Readings are --:</u>

       * educational
       * fun to perform
       * require no memorizing
       * require few props, and are
       * for use in classrooms,
         retreats, Women's History
         Month programs, lay-led
         services, etc.

Whenever possible *(to be sure of pronunciations and format)*, have readers go over the scripts before the program or class presentation.
Caution readers to speak **loudly** and **clearly** so that everyone can hear them.

The study of history is useful
to the (male) historian by teaching him
his ignorance of women; and the mass of this ignorance crushes one
who is familiar enough with what are called historical sources
to realize how few women have ever been known. The woman who is
known only through men is known wrong....

—Henry Brooks Adams
1898
The Education of Adams
(Silence)

Introduction

These short dramatic readings are for use in classrooms, for lay-led services, and for public programs, such as Women's History Month *(March)* as well as for personal leisure reading.

Each dramatic reading requires two to six readers, only a few props *(if any),* and no memorizing. Before a public presentation, it is wise to go over the reading*(s)* to be sure of pronunciations and timing. Caution readers to speak loudly and clearly.

Because two readings **(Harriet Ross Tubman** and **George Sand)** focus on extraordinary women of courage and commitment, they make ideal programs for groups such as OWL, NOW, WILPF, AAUW, LWV, and NWSA.*

* *Older Women's League, National Organization for Women, Women's International League for Peace and Freedom, American Association of University Women, League of Women Voters, National Women's Studies Association.*

Although these dramatic readings capture the essence of each woman's contributions to social change, it is hoped that they will pique interest and spark discussions so that audiences/students become motivated to seek additional knowledge.

Lilith: Adam's First Wife is an ideal program for Unitarian Universalist lay-led services and groups (UUWF, CUUPS, W&R*) as well as classes in religion and philosophy.

Lilith: Adam's First Wife**

Lilith is an ancient transition myth. It reflects the transition from the time when women were held in high esteem and the idea of goddesses was universal to recent historical times when women were suppressed by men who used the idea of gods *(and then one almighty male god)* to destroy ancient goddess worship and establish patriarchy.

In the 1940s, I lived in a small town in North Dakota with a population under 3,000. There were a half-dozen or more churches in this farming community and my parents were the pillars of the little Methodist church. One Sunday, when I was about 13, I quietly moved to the back pew in order to surreptitiously polish my fingernails.

As I listened to the minister *(a portly, friendly old man)* tell a biblical story that made no logical sense, I remember thinking, "This is nonsense. A person would have to be stupid or crazy to believe this story." I looked around at the

---

* *Unitarian Universalist Women's Federation; Covenant of Unitarian Universalist Pagans; Women & Religion.*
** *The idea of marriage was unknown during prehistoric times. The word wife, from OE (wif) means woman/worker, e.g. fish wif, midwif, housewif....*

seated adults, people I had assumed were smart, and asked myself, "How can grown ups believe these fairy tales? Don't they know that the Easter Bunny, Santa Claus, angels, devils, and gods are make believe?"

I became an instant atheist. Since then, my rejection of organized religions and superstitions has been repeatedly confirmed. After becoming a feminist, I learned how patriarchal religions *(including Judaism/Christianity/Islam)* doomed women to inequality, low status, rape, incest, sexual harassment, battery, female genital mutilation, bound feet, suttee, forced marriages, unwanted pregnancies, lives of drudgery, ad infinitum.

When I first heard the story of **Lilith**, I exclaimed, "Aha, here is an ancient transition myth; a story of the transition from a time of goddess worship when women were independent and held in high esteem to the time patriarchy emerged and used religion to force women into servant status."

In this dramatic reading, I have used the format of having **Ancient Lilith** return to inform a **Modern Lilith** what *really* "went down" in the Garden of Eden story, to set the record straight, and to urge modern feminists *(Liliths)* and more traditional women *(Eves)* to work together in order to make the world a paradise again.

Yes, **Ancient Lilith** is self-centered and uppity, but she is not the evil demon depicted through the centuries by Judaism and Christianity.

There was a time when men not only worshipped *(valued or gave worth to)* females, but feared them, too. If a woman can spread her legs and magically give birth *(to both females and males)*, surely she has the power to bring death. Lilith was demonized as a baby killer and one who brings death, as well as one who causes men *(especially priests and monks)* to have wet dreams.

The **Lilith** myth has been interpreted in many ways. I view it as explaining a time when women were *not* doormats, a time when birth and Springtime, the development of agriculture and the domestication of animals were magical; a time focused on females and fertility. When our ancestors learned that the cow could not get pregnant without the bull, the woman without the seed of a male, some men took power, creating the concept of private property and control over women, children, concubines, harems, slaves, as well as all the animals and the Earth itself. It took thousands of years to destroy the old goddess religions, create a "power over" paradigm, and relegate women to subservient status.

Patriarchs blamed women for all pain, sin and death. Indeed, all personal and social problems were blamed on women via simplistic Garden of Eve stories, e.g. humans once lived in a Utopia, then Eve disobeyed the one all-powerful new male god so people were kicked out of the Garden of Plenty and thus have had to work and suffer ever since. Original Sin was the primary ammunition used to subjugate women to the authority of church, state, and men, and became an excuse for torturing and murdering hundreds of thousands of women during the Inquisition and the witch-hunts-- the Burning Times. Eve was disobedient so women are potentially disobedient creatures who can lead men into sin; don't ever trust a woman. Because the mythical Eve ate from the Tree of Knowledge, women must henceforth and forever suffer not only in childbirth but in all aspects of life. Unfortunately, this has been, and is, the lot of most women.

There are numerous readings to accompany the dramatic reading **Lilith: Adam's First Wife**, including the poems *"Prunings From The Garden of Eden"* by Shirley Trout Josephson, *"Ishtar"* by Helen Szymkowiak, *"Read Between the Lines,"* and *"Look For Me."*

Other options are readings such as *"A 10-Minute History of Patriarchy," "St. Patrick's Day," "May Day," "5 Ways to Kill People,"* and/or responsive readings, such as *"It Is Good To Remember"* and *"To Acknowledge Our Ancestors."* Readings to close your program include *"Benediction," "Becoming,"* and *"Sojourners."*

I am indebted to Elizabeth Fisher and Mary F. Heath who presented a "feminar"* on **Lilith** at a Unitarian Universalist women's retreat. Mary was kind enough to critique the dramatic reading and many of her suggestions have been incorporated into **Lilith: Adam's First Wife**. Thanks also to Sally Reed for sharing her paper on **Lilith** and to Joys Angel for her suggestions.

You brilliant women bring knowledge and love to our world; I treasure you!

Moon Goddess is a reading for 13 female voices. Women stand in a circle — each reading one segment, each gathering strength and empowerment from the others. You may wish to use this during an outdoor moon ritual, using candles or flashlights to facilitate the reading.

---

*   *The words seminar and seminary come from the word seminal, pertaining to sperm or seed — so we had a 'feminar'!*

Dorothy Satir, who lives in San Francisco, wrote **Circle of Sisterhood** for a Women & Religion Task Force retreat *(Pacific Central District, Unitarian Universalist Association).* Her message is that we can <u>choose</u> women friends to be our sisters. It is short *(about 10 minutes)* and the number of readers can vary from two to five *(it is written for five readers).*

<u>**Feelings**</u> is a dramatic reading for six readers — three female and three male. It is based on a story by Rod Walter *(who died March 17, 1995).* After presenting this dramatic reading, use the character Fred and his violence to elicit discussion on why so many men are **not** in touch with their feelings.

George Sand: Deviant Extraordinaire

As with most historical women, **George Sand** *(1804-1876)* was not part of my formal education. As a teacher, I discovered that students knew little, if anything, about this gifted 19th century French novelist and playwright.*

Born Aurore Dupin in 1804, she fled an unhappy marriage, cross-dressed, smoked cigars, had numerous affairs *(mostly with weak sickly men, such as Frederic Chopin),* used the male pseudonym of George Sand in order to get published, wrote over 100 volumes of prose — close to 60 novels, 25 plays *(all staged),* autobiographies, letters and essays in order to support countless people *(including several children, two of her own)* and became the most popular, charitable, and controversial author in Europe.

* <u>*Question:*</u> *Do you know who George Sand was?*
<u>*Answer:*</u> *No, who was* **he?**

xviii

Aurore was only four when her aristocratic father died from a horseback riding accident; her beloved grandmother died when Aurore was 16; her mother was mentally unstable; her husband and half-brother were alcoholics; most of her lovers required nurturing and financial support; her headstrong daughter gave her nothing but trouble and heartache; and her son adored her. **George Sand** was a multidimensional woman, a Romantic who lived her life with one crisis after another. Her life exceeded the imagination of her pen.

In this dramatic reading, **George Sand**, 70, reflects on her tempestuous life in a casual discussion with her beloved son, Maurice, 52. It is the year 1875, the year before her unexpected death.

Harriet Ross Tubman

If I had the power, every city in the United States would have a statue of **Harriet Tubman** *(1820?- 1913)*. Yes, I would replace all those old statues of military men on horseback that glorify war with statues of women, such as the heroic **Harriet Ross Tubman.**

Harriet Ross was born into a loving slave family on a Maryland plantation around 1820. She was treated cruelly as a child and almost died when struck on the forehead with an iron bar by an overseer; the blow resulted in spells of narcolepsy *(falling asleep for varied time periods)*. When her husband, John Tubman, refused to escape with her to Freedomland *(Pennsylvania)*, Harriet went alone. She felt that she had "a right to freedom or death, and if I can't have one, I will have the other."

She couldn't rest knowing that her family and others were still in slavery; she had "heard their moans" and despite spells of narcolepsy, illiteracy, a distinctive scar on her forehead, and slave owners offering a $40,000.* reward for her capture, dead or alive, she made 10 trips back South to lead over 300 people to freedom — all the way to Canada after the Fugitive Slave Act of 1850.

Harriet Ross Tubman is the only known woman to have planned and led military expeditions during the Civil War; she was also a nurse, spy, and scout for the Union *(North)*. Although always poor, after the Civil War she managed to open a Home for Old Coloured Folks in Auburn, New York.

In this dramatic reading the year is 1901. An imaginary reporter interviews **Ms. Tubman** in the backyard of her home; she is about 80 years old.

Also included in this book is a chant and several poems and readings, including Responsive Readings. Feel free to use any of these to expand your program or presentation.

I think that dramatic readings are a wonderful way to explore history, analyze social problems, and exchange ideas.

Enjoy!

Meg Bowman
1996

* *About $700,000. in 1990s dollars.*

LILITH:

ADAM'S FIRST WIFE

A TRANSITION MYTH

by

Meg Bowman

1

Many thanks
to
Mary F. Heath,
Sally Reed,
Jean Embree,
Naomi Sherer,
and
Joys Angel
for their ideas
and
editing.

—*Meg Bowman*

2

There was a time when you were not a slave, remember that. You walked alone, full of laughter, you bathed bare-bellied.
You say you have lost all recollection of it, remember....
You say there are no words to describe this time, you say it does not exist.

But remember.
Make an effort to remember.
Or, failing that, invent.

—Monique Wittig, **Les Guerilleres**
(NY: Bard Book/Avon, 1963/73)
p. 89. *Translated from the French by David Le Vay.* Viking Press, 1971.
Beacon Press *edition, 1985.*

Lilith

The disturbing Lilith... being the most dangerous and subversive threat to the established male order, was buried in the furthest depths of the Hebrew unconscious.

—Jean Markale

The story of the Garden of Eden

is an echo

of a Golden Age.

WHO IS LILITH?

<u>Semitic mythology:</u> Lilith was the first wife of Adam. She is depicted on an ancient plaque (ca. 2000-2300 B.C.E.) as a beautiful, naked young woman with wings and the feet of a bird, probably an owl. Most of the traditions about her come to us from Talmudic/Midrashic literature and from folklore. Lilith is best known for her role in Jewish/Hebrew tradition, but her roots go back to an earlier Sumerian religious epic. She became a demonized figure, often shown as a composite of woman and bird/animal, known for unbidden sexual activity and baby-stealing. Her associations are with animals, owls, the desert, sexuality, the moon, darkness, and death.

—Mary F. Heath

Lilith and Eve

LILITH:

ADAM'S FIRST WIFE

Dramatic Reading

for

Three Readers

Meg Bowman

7

NOTE:

So that audiences can identify with Modern Lilith, a fictional character reminiscent of the research psychologist character depicted in the television series "Cheers" was created; Ancient Lilith is based on numerous Lilith mythology resources *(see References and Bibliography)*.

Both characters are, of course, fictional.

LILITH: ADAM'S FIRST WIFE

DRAMATIC READING FOR
THREE READERS

CAST:

1) Ancient Lilith: Mythical first wife of Adam.
Dressed in a long flowing caftan
or robe or gown, she carries an owl
(clay or cloth stuffed toy).

She is strong, self-reliant and wise.

2) Modern Lilith: Dressed in modern attire, perhaps in
a business suit. Her dark hair can be
pulled back in an austere style. She
is brilliant and inquisitive; a no-
nonsense modern woman.

3) Voice Off Stage: Person with a strong voice.
Can be male or female.

PROPS:

Two chairs and, if desired, a TV set.

One ceramic or toy cloth stuffed owl.

Note:
Remind readers to speak
loudly and clearly.

Opening: Modern Lilith is seated, watching TV.

VOICE OFF STAGE:

Who was Lilith?

In Semitic mythology she was the first wife of Adam.

One myth says* : In the beginning were formed Adam and Lilith created from the same substance, equal in all ways.

Adam, man that he was, didn't like it. He said, "Lilith, I'll have my figs now" ordering her to wait on him, but Lilith wasn't one to take orders and flew away.

"Well," complained Adam to God, "that uppity woman you sent has deserted me."

Lilith, preferring **anything** to living with Adam, was happy living with the animals.

So Eve was created and Adam was happy with his helper.

Adam told Eve fearsome stories making a demon of Lilith, but when Lilith came back to the Garden, Eve saw that Lilith was a woman much like herself.

---

* *See "Epilogue: The Coming of Lilith"* by Judith Plaskow Goldenberg with Karen Bloomquist, Margaret Early, and Elizabeth Farians, Religion and Sexism: Images of Women in the Jewish and Christian Traditions.

11

Seeds of curiosity and doubt began
to grow in Eve's mind.

How beautiful and strong Lilith looked!

How bravely she had talked back to Adam!

Eve decided it was time to eat from the
Tree of Knowledge....[1]   Aha!

Do you know what **really** happened in that
Garden of Eden?

Why Eve was framed?

Why Lilith was written out of history?

Let's discover what **really** "went down"
in that Garden.

Many of you have watched the television comedy
"Cheers" *(now in re-runs)* and recognize the
character of Lilith, the research psychologist
once married to Frasier.

Let's listen as a modern Lilith receives a visit
from the ancient Lilith, the first woman—
Adam's first wife.

MODERN LILITH: (TALKING TO HERSELF;
                          WATCHING TV)

There goes Frasier....
into Cheers again.

(SIGHS IN DISGUST)

Oh, that man....

(PUZZLED)

Hmmmmm....
No one ever seems to get drunk
in that bar.
Hmmmmmmmm....
Why do people watch
mindless television?

(SIGHS)

Another re-run.
(PAUSE)

Honestly, Frasier....

(SHAKES HEAD NEGATIVELY)

My husband is such a jerk....

LILITH: (OFF STAGE)

                     Mine, too. I left the turkey!

MODERN LILITH: (STARTLED)
                     Who said that?
                     Who's there?

LILITH: (OFF STAGE)

                     I did. The first Lilith.

                     (ENTERS STAGE CARRYING
                     AN OWL ARTIFACT)

                     Hello, Lilith.
                     We not only have the same name,
                     we both have husband problems.
                     I left mine.

MODERN LILITH: Am I having a visual hallucination?

LILITH: Please don't be frightened.
                     My name is Lilith, just like
                     your name.

MODERN LILITH: Why are you here?

14

LILITH: To set the record straight.
                        Do you remember the Adam and
                        Eve story?

                        Well, I'm Adam's **first** wife.

MODERN LILITH: Come again?

LILITH: I am the first woman, Lilith,
                        your namesake.
                        I am an ancient goddess.
                        I am Lilith, Angel of the Night.

MODERN LILITH: Why are you dressed
                        so strangely?

LILITH: At least I have clothes on....
                        Have you seen the ancient plaque,
                        the one made of clay, depicting me
                        nude—**but beautiful**—with wings
                        and the feet of a bird?

MODERN LILITH: No. I've never even **heard**
                        of you.
                        It sounded like you said Lilith....
                        That's my name, too.
                        You say **your** name is Lilith?

15

LILITH: I don't expect you to know
                     who I am.

MODERN LILITH: You got that right.

LILITH: I am Lilith, Angel of the Night.
                     The literal meaning of Lilith is
                     "WIND, SPIRIT."

                     I am the spirit of independent
                     women.

MODERN LILITH: (INCREDULOUS)

                     And you're the first woman?

LILITH: Sure am!
                     You know the Adam and Eve story.
                     Well, in Jewish history, I'm the first
                     wife of Adam....

                     The Talmud (TAHL' MUD)
                     describes me as a "charming
                     woman."

To the Canaanites (KAIN-AH-NITES) I was **Baalat** (BAY-LOT), the "Divine Lady," and the Arabs called me "The **Holy** Lady."

Oh, I'm **in** Midrashic (MID'-RASH-IC) literature, too.

The Cabbala (KAH'-BAH-LAH) writings say I taught **wisdom** to Adam....

MODERN LILITH: What are you doing here?
You must be thousands of years old!

LILITH: I'm from way back in Old Babylonia....
more than 4,000 years ago!

I come from a Sumerian epic.
I was worshipped as the Queen of Heaven **before** Inanna (IH'-NAH-'NAH).

I filled their wells and rivers with water.

Have you heard of the Goddess Inanna, or Nana (NAN-AH) or Anna, Queen of the Universe?

17

MODERN LILITH: No. Oh, there were many
gods and goddesses in
ancient times, like, uh, uh....

LILITH: Babylonians called me Ishtar.
A "star."
In the Bible, I am the Great Goddess
Ashtoreth (ASH'-TOR-ETH),
highest of the World, Righteous
Judge, Most Awesome, Most
Powerful!

MODERN LILITH: Wow!

LILITH: When people learned agriculture
and I fertilized the land, the Hitites
worshipped me as Inaras (IN-AR'-
AS).

MODERN LILITH: Well, goddesses never were
a part of **my** education.

LILITH: When men and their gods took
power, goddess worship was
doomed.

It's a sad story, Lilith—one of
hatred, terror, death....

18

MODERN LILITH: I certainly want to hear this.
                  Here, sit down.
                  (MOTIONS TO CHAIR)

                  Can I get you a cold drink....
                  after your long....uh... journey?

LILITH: (SITTING)

                  No, thanks.*

                  My story tells how women became
                  scorned and hated...
                   I shudder at the terror....
                  It's the story of the transition
                   from ancient Goddess worship
                   to male gods.

MODERN LILITH: **That's** heavy.
                  But, what are you doing here?

LILITH: I want to let you know that you have
                  a namesake.
                  I also want to set the record straight.
                  Our name 'Lilith' has been maligned
                  much too long.

<u>OPTION</u>: Thank you.
      (MODERN LILITH pours her a drink.)

19

MODERN LILITH: I've wondered what the
name Lilith meant.

You say the origin of our
name is "WIND" and "SPIRIT"?

LILITH: Yes. And the flower of **Lilith** in
ancient times was the lily, the "lilu"
or lotus of the genital magic.

MODERN LILITH: Genital magic, eh?
Is that why you have a lily
embroidered on your garment?

LILITH: The lily was sacred to Astarte (AH'-
STAR'-TAY), one of my **many**
goddess names.

Northern Europeans called me
Ostara or Eostre (ES-TRAH).

Voila! (VWAH-LAH') Easter! [2]

MODERN LILITH: The Easter lily!

LILITH: Genital magic also means virgin
motherhood.

20

Hey, how's this for a myth?

The lily in Gabriel's hand filtered
God's semen which entered Mary
through her ear!?[3]

MODERN LILITH: I have heard that virgin
births were popular in Egypt,
China....among Aztecs [4]
... several thousand years ago.

But getting pregnant through one's
ear?!

LILITH: That's why women were required
to wear scarves while in church.
Men such as Paul, Josephus (JO-
SEE'FUS), Philo (FY-LO),
Tertullian (TER-TOO'-LEE-ON)
and even Martin Luther were con-
vinced that both angels and demons
entered women through the ears.

MODERN LILITH: Such nonsense!

LILITH: People have always believed
in myths.

21

My myth goes back to Mesopotamia
(MESS-O'-PAH-TAY'-ME-AH)—
the creation story.

Well, **one** of the creation stories.

MODERN LILITH: We all know the myth of Adam
 and Eve.
But no one ever told me that
Adam had a **first** wife.

LILITH: Yup, that's me.

My roots go back to an early
Sumerian epic poem, but when
I dumped old Adam and flew away,
I was demonized....

Depicted as part woman/part
bird.... usually an owl.

(HOLDS UP OWL AND THEN
PLACES THE ARTIFACT ON
THE FLOOR BY HER CHAIR)

I hover over the earth.

I speak the truth and "see in the
dark."

Yes, I am clear-sighted even in eras
of darkness, ignorance, superstition,
wrong-thinking...

MODERN LILITH: Well, owls **are** said to be wise.

Tell me about Adam?
Was he like Frasier?

LILITH: When making love, does Frasier
insist that you lie on your back
with him on top? [5]

MODERN LILITH: **This** is why you left Adam?

LILITH: One of the reasons.
I refused to lie below him
while making love.
He refused to be below me.

He said, "You are fit to be below me
and I above you." I insisted,
"We are **both** equal because we
both come from the earth."

We argued.
We argued **a lot**!

MODERN LILITH: Well, Lilith, we **both** cherish
our freedom.
I don't take domination
from Frasier or from any man!

And I cherish **my** autonomy.

LILITH: Me, too, and I **knew** my power.
I asserted my rights;
voiced my opinions.

Then, uttered an oath
and flew away!

Left the Garden of Eden and
went to live with the animals.

MODERN LILITH: Where did you go?

LILITH: I flew to the shores of the Red Sea,
back to my Moon Goddess
cultures.... the wilderness.

Adam missed me and had Yahweh
(YAH-WAY) send three angels—
Sen, San and Sam *   —something
like that— to fetch me back.

* *Senoi, Sansenoi and Samangloph.*

24

Hah! No way!

I was having a grand time producing children— (BRAGGING) over a hundred a day!

MODERN LILITH: (INCREDULOUS)
No way!

LILITH: Men were just taking power then, so when I "flew the coop" you can imagine the negative stories told about me!

MODERN LILITH: What did they say?

LILITH: First, they threatened to kill my children.

(ANGRY)

I **should** have been a symbol for women's wisdom/power/ independence, but **no**, those old patriarchs threatened me and then claimed that when children died, **I** was to blame....

25

MODERN LILITH: How awful!

LILITH: Finally, they said I could stay,
but only with this restriction:
I must **never** harm a newborn child
who wore an amulet (AM'-U-LET)
that bore the three angels' names
or images.

MODERN LILITH: Great for the amulet
business, eh?

LILITH: Indeed.
Those old men had the audacity
to blame me for **all** miscarriages,
stillbirths, and infant deaths.
I was seen as **most** dangerous to **boy**
babies, who were vulnerable to me
until they were eight years old.

Girl babies were out of danger
after 20 days.

MODERN LILITH: How long did this craziness go on?

26

LILITH: Those guys sold amulets
                     for centuries!
                     Incantation formulas to protect
                     women in childbirth abounded
                     in Assyria.

                     In northern Syria people still sing
                     (CHANTS) *"...to hear that which
                     flies in rooms of darkness—pass
                     quickly, quickly, Lilith."*

                     I **love** babies and would never harm
                     a single one, but by the Middle
                     Ages, I was a demon.... so they said.

MODERN LILITH: Did they actually call you a demon?

LILITH: Not only that, they believed
                     I had great powers as a seducer!

                     Men feared I would take their
                     "essence," their precious seed.
                     Throughout the centuries, male
                     clergy have hated me.

                     They made me a monster who
                     visited men at night and caused
                     them to be sterile or impotent.

They said my daughters—
all beautiful—called "lilim"—
tortured men in their sleep and
caused nocturnal emissions.

It was said that every time a
Christian monk had a wet dream,
Lilith laughed.

(LAUGHS)

They used to sleep clutching
a crucifix with their hands
on their genitals.

MODERN LILITH: Our name is **still** tainted.
Back when Cabbage Patch
dolls were a fad, I heard
of a woman who returned one
to a store because it was
named Linda Lilith

LILITH: Yup, negative stories *(are)*
still around.
Just because I refused to participate
in their domination over women.

MODERN LILITH: But, Lilith, why haven't
                  I ever heard of you?

LILITH: Judaism and Christianity
                  just wrote me out....barely
                  a mention anywhere.
                  First, Eve and I were blamed
                  for **everything.**

                  Then, the focus was on Eve.
                  When she rebelled and ate from
                   the Tree of Knowledge, they really
                  did a number on her.

MODERN LILITH: Did you ever talk to Eve?

LILITH: Indeed.

                  It was I, Lilith, who urged Eve to
                  rebel.

                  You see, I was totally **un**acceptable
                  to those emerging Hebrew patriarchs
                  so.... Eve was invented— subordi-
                  nate, obedient, no real power, sexu-
                  ally confined to procreation— but
                  she rebelled against dictatorship.

MODERN LILITH: So, did you go back to the
Garden of Eden?

LILITH: Sure did.
Eve saw me and we talked
a long time.
I encouraged Eve to leave
the Garden.
"Be independent, Eve," I said.
"Empower yourself. You have
choices —we women should stick
together."

MODERN LILITH: Oh, Lilith, with you and Eve
working together, we could
have had Utopia in the world.

LILITH: I told Eve we were very much alike,
both strong women.

I told her that Adam was making her
a servant, a prostitute.... ashamed
of her womanhood.

MODERN LILITH: What did she say?

LILITH: Adam had told her terrible stories
                         about me, **but** she saw that I was
                         a woman like her.

                         She said I was beautiful and so
                         brave to talk back to Adam.

                         But, she wouldn't come with me....

MODERN LILITH: There are still lots of Eves
                         in the world.

LILITH: ....and they're still warned about
                         the **two** forbidden trees:
                         the Tree of Life.... **my tree**,
                         and the Tree of Knowledge.

MODERN LILITH: Well, didn't a snake come along
                         and tell Eve that her eyes would be
                         opened if she went ahead and ate
                         from the Tree of Knowledge? [6]

LILITH: Eve saw that the tree was good,
                         a delight to the eyes... *"that the tree
                         was desired to make one wise and
                         she took of its fruit and ate."*

31

MODERN LILITH: I don't see anything wrong with
that! She chose to seek wisdom
rather than blind obedience.

What was this other tree,
the Tree of Life?

LILITH: Remember, Lilith, these are
myths from the time when people
worshipped female/fertility/feminine
symbols.

The Tree of Life is an ancient
Sumerian tradition.... long before
Judaism and the Sky God that
blamed Eve for death[7] and all
the evil in the world.

MODERN LILITH: I remember seeing a painting
once — of a special tree
in the Garden of Eden.

An owl was in the tree and a serpent
was at the bottom of the tree.

LILITH: That was the Tree of Life....
I lived there with the wise old owl.
The snake was a symbol for the
ancient goddess, Inanna, **me**!

MODERN LILITH: Well, I **don't** like snakes
                   but they have certainly played
                   prominent roles in ancient myths.

                   Doesn't take a degree in psychology
                   to figure out the messages—:

                   The snake, symbolizing ancient
                   goddess religions, became evil.

LILITH: Yes, and the original Great Goddess
                   had to be dethroned in order for
                   male gods to take over.

MODERN LILITH: So, Eve eats from the Tree of
                   Knowledge, gives some to Adam
                   and, realizing they're naked, feel
                   ashamed, so they cover themselves
                   with fig leaves or Fruit of the Loom
                   or whatever.

LILITH: Oh, and **sex** is now sinful.

MODERN LILITH: Religious zealots often have weird
                   sexual hang-ups.
                    Ever watch those TV evangelists?

LILITH: And when Eve disobeyed Yahweh
                     (YAH-WAY), they blamed **her**
                     for human suffering and death.

MODERN LILITH: So they managed to project their
                     fear of death onto women?

LILITH: Blamed it all on Eve. See what
                     happens when women disobey?

MODERN LILITH: Those old men said Eve had exposed
                     them to death so they **had to** put a
                     curse on **all** women.

LILITH: People bought this story,
                     hook-line-and-sinker!

MODERN LILITH: Well, it does explain some of our
                     attitudes about suffering, death,
                     gender roles, shame about our
                     bodies...
                     (PAUSE)
                     Hmmm....

                     So, Adam and Eve were
                     kicked out of the Garden?

LILITH: Given the boot!

MODERN LILITH: Obviously a patriarchal ploy.
                     Talk about being **framed!**
                     Poor Eve.

LILITH: Adam blamed Eve, Eve blamed the
                     snake, and the Sky God cursed
                     them all.

                     The Bible said women **must** suffer.

MODERN LILITH: Yes, submit to your husband and
                     suffer in childbirth.

                     Even after chloroform was invented
                     in the 19th century, men refused to
                     give anesthesia to women in labor.

LILITH: Women's sexuality was controlled—
                     we were segregated into women's
                     quarters, chaperoned, veiled,
                     genitally mutilated, sexually
                     harassed, stalked, beaten, stoned
                     to death, starved, raped, bought and
                     sold...   married off....

MODERN LILITH: (INCENSED)

It's still going on today!

LILITH: Then, good old Paul, the super
salesman, incorporated this story
into the heart of Christian myth as
the story of "the fall" of humanity.

Ah, if only Eve and I had taken
more time to talk and tell our stories,
to laugh together, and to cry, and to
strengthen our bond of Sisterhood.

MODERN LILITH: Perhaps it's not too late. Although
relationships between women —
and relationships between men
and women — have certainly been
poisoned.

LILITH: People still fear independent
women, and the sexuality of
a Lilith.

MODERN LILITH: Well, Frasier and I have had
our share of problems.

LILITH: Everyone, women **and** men, need
                       to connect with our feminine traits;
                       we all need to nurture one another,
                       our world, the animals....

MODERN LILITH: And speak out.

LILITH: Ah, my namesake, women **are**
                       finally speaking out, making
                       demands, becoming Sisters,
                       getting educated.... that Tree
                       of Knowledge **will** set us free.

MODERN LILITH: Women must tell one another
                       their stories.
                       I guess changes will really come
                       when the Eves and the Liliths
                       of the world come together and
                       rebuild the Garden....

                       I think Frasier will help, too.

LILITH: Forget Adam! That die-hard
                       will never change.

MODERN LILITH: Well, we Liliths of the world
                       are ready!

LILITH: It is time to set the record straight. It is time for women to be **once again** independent.

MODERN LILITH: Time to throw off feelings of inferiority, feelings of powerlessness, feelings of guilt.

LILITH: We must reclaim our autonomy, our name....

MODERN LILITH: We **are** powerful, independent, and wise....we **do** hover over the earth.

LILITH: We are like owls in the wilderness. We see in the dark. We are clear-sighted in eras of darkness and ignorance....

(STANDS AND PICKS UP OWL FROM THE FLOOR)

The wise ones.
The uppity ones.
The brave ones.

MODERN LILITH: (STANDS)

Our name, **Lilith,** is a symbol
for independent thinking—
for women's voices.

It is time to make the world
a Garden of Eden again.

It is time to know that we are related
to all living things.... to the Earth
itself.

LILITH: (HOLDS LILITH'S HAND)

Body, mind and spirit **are**
inseparable.
Come, Lilith, fly on the wind
with me.
We move with the strength
of the wind.

At night, we see clearly when
others are lost in darkness.

With wisdom, knowing our past,
we can help to shape the future.

We are nocturnal wind specters.
Wind/Spirit/Breath/Earth/Life/
Freedom.

39

(THE TWO WOMEN HOLD
HANDS AND SAY TOGETHER
WHILE EXITING)

BOTH WOMEN: We are the Wind; we are the Spirit
                  of the Future.

                  Wind/Spirit. Wind/Spirit.

                  (EXIT)

VOICE OFF STAGE: *Read all (or only the last
                  three paragraphs--see p. 42):*

                  Who was Lilith?

                  In ancient Babylonian-Assyrian/
                  Sumerian language the word for
                  wind *(spirit)* was **lilitu** (LIL-AH-
                  TU).

                  In Semitic mythology, Lilith was
                  the first wife of Adam.

                  Her roots go back to an earlier
                  Sumerian religious epic.

She represents the spirit
of independent women.

She was an ancient goddess
at a time when women had status
and people honored the feminine.

Lilith represents the transition
from matrifocal cultures and Goddess worship to patriarchal societies
with their male god or gods.

Lilith represents female autonomy.

The winged Lilith is a strong role
model for modern women —
womenwho need encouragement
to leave unhealthy relationships —
womenwho need to feel strong
and self-reliant.

Monotheistic religions demonized
Lilith —the uppity, independent
woman who dumped Adam and
went to live with the animals.

Later, she returned to the Garden
of Eden and tried to talk Eve into
leaving, too.

The patriarchs had a fit!

Lilith was an uppity woman who
refused to succumb to male power
so she was called a screeching night
owl who kills babies, a demon....
and Lilith was then written out
of patriarchal history.

***

It is time to remember Lilith, symbol
of freedom. It is time for Eve and
Lilith to talk and tell their stories.
It is time for the Eves and the Liliths
of the world to come together.

It is time to celebrate the power
of women's friendships.

It is time....

OPTION # 1:   Thank you, Modern Lilith and
                     Ancient Lilith.

                     Wind/Spirit/Breath/Earth/Life/
                     Freedom, please fly back to us now
                     and take a bow.

OPTION #2:   Wind/Spirit/Breath/Earth/Life/
                     Freedom.

                     Will all the uppity Liliths in the
                     audience please stand as Modern
                     Lilith and Ancient Lilith fly back to
                     us now to take their bow?

                     Thank you.

                     (MODERN LILITH AND
                     ANCIENT LILITH RETURN
                     FOR A CURTAIN CALL THUS
                     SIGNALING THE END
                     OF THE DRAMATIC READING.)

REFERENCES:

1 Adapted from **Epilogue: The Coming of Lilith**, Judith Plaskow
Goldenberg, *with* Karen Bloomquist, Margaret Early, *and* Elizabeth
Farians *printed in* **Religion and Sexism: Images of Woman in the
Jewish and Christian Traditions** *(NY: Simon & Shuster, 1974),
pp. 341-343.*

*2 The goddess Oestre/Eostre gave birth to the words estrogen and
estrus. Easter shows its pagan origin in a dating system based on the
old lunar calendar: it is fixed as the first Sunday after the first full
moon after the Spring Equinox. The Christian festival wasn't called
Easter until the Goddess' name was given to it in the late Middle Ages.*

*3 Celts and others called the virgin mother Lily Maid. In France her
magic yonic/pelvic emblem was the fleur-de-lis. White caps worn by
nurses and nuns were originally shaped to represent a lily. The story
of the Virgin Mary being impregnated by the "holy ghost" via her ear
did not emerge until the 4th century and was followed by the story of
her being raped by the angel Gabriel who received the "immaculate
sperm upon his coat sleeve" which he blew down Mary's windpipe, in
the form of a vapor. See* Henry Ziboorg & Geo. W. Henry, **History of
Medical Psychology,** *(NY: Hicton, 1941).*

*4 The Aztec goddess Coatlicue was supposedly impregnated by a
floating feather which resulted in the birth of the war god, Huitzilop-
pochtli. The popularity of virgin births is described in* **Women, Food
and Sex, Vol. I,** *Soledad De Montalvo, (American Atheist Press,
Austin, TX, 1988) , p. 45.*
*"Lacking vaginas, many gods gave birth from their mouths," e.g.
priests of Ra (Egypt). Atum (local god of Helopolis, Greece) gave
birth to the primal couple from his penis by masturbation. Norsemen
claimed the first male-and-female were born from the sweaty armpit of
Ymir.*
*"The idea for Adam's magic birth-giving came from a Sumerian
childbirth-goddess, Nin-Ti 'Lady of the Rib' -- the word Ti meant both
Life and Rib."*
After Zeus gave birth to the much older Athena from his forehead, he

*gave birth to Dionysus from his thigh. Apollo sat on eggs trying to
copy the life-giving magic of his mother who gave birth to the world.
In Egypt, the mother of the World Egg was Hathor in the guise of the
Nile Goose--hence, the Goose Who Laid the Golden Egg.
Early Christians evolved "birth rites" claiming men could impregnate
each other by kissing. Christianity demoted the Goddess to mortal
status of both Eve and Mary. Gnostic Gospels said Adam came into
being from the Virgin Earth, who was none other than Eve. The story
of her birth from Adam was a late, distorted version of the myth.
See* Barbara G. Walker, ***The Woman's Encyclopedia of Myths and
Secrets,*** *(Harper & Row, San Francisco, 1983) pp. 106-109.*

*The Biblical story of Adam's rib undergoes a curious inversion when
told by the Mudurucu (of Brazil). Their version is that when
Karusakaibo made the women out of clay, he gave one to each man.
He had, however, made one too many, and, to make a husband for the
extra woman, he took one of <u>her</u> ribs while she slept and made it into a
man; their names were Adjun and Eva.* **<u>Women of the Forest,</u>** Yolanda
and Robert Murphy, *p. 104.*

*5 Catholic authorities decreed any sexual position other than the
male-superior one as sinful.* Larousse, ***Encyclopedia of Mythology***
(London: Hamlyn, 1968), p. 202.

6 "The ancient Aegean world worshipped primarily women and
serpents." "*Serpent of the Nile* was the title, not only of Cleopatra, but
of all Egyptian queens..." "...the serpent was worshipped in Palestine
long before Yahweh's cult rose." See Walker, <u>*Op. cit.,*</u> *pp. 903-909.*

7 *"The Book of Enoch said God created death to punish all humanity
for Eve's sin, but many patriarchal thinkers hesitated to blame God
even indirectly. The prevalent opinion was that when Eve disobeyed
the deity, death somehow just happened. Paul blamed only Eve,
absolving Adam from guilt for the apple-eating incident.*
　　*"Adam was not deceived, but the woman being deceived was in the
transgression" (1 Timothy 2:14). A church council announced in 418
C.E. that it was heresy to say death was a natural necessity rather
than the result of Eve's disobedience."* Walker, <u>*Op. cit.,*</u> *p. 290.*

....tradition from the dawn of time says that the ultimate creative principle-- the power that most people call God-- manifests itself in two aspects: the god and the goddess. Of these, He is that which energizes and fertilizes; She is that which forms and nourishes. From their unity springs all activity, all life, all creation.

In this tradition (which is shared by magicians, mystics, and witches), all gods are one god, and all goddesses one goddess. Apollo, Osiris, Allah, Jehovah are but faces of Him. Aphrodite, Isis, Diana, Mary are but the forms in which we clothe Her.

The Serpent of Lilith
Margot Villiers
Pocket Books, New York (1976)
Forward

46

LOOK FOR ME

Look for me—
  I am Lilith
  Who never died
  The wise owl
  Who never lied

Look for me—
  I am the wisdom
  of the Owl and the Moon
  The Goddess who fled
  Adam's certain ruin
Ages and ages old
Damned for being free and bold

I see in the darkest night
I dwell within your sight
I am brilliant flowing light
  Ever changing
  Always sustaining
  Growing bright

Look for me.

—*Meg Bowman*

47

The Burney Relief; terracotta plaque of Lilith, aka Inanna-Ishtar, with lions, owls and the rod and line of measurement; c. 2300-2000 B.C.E.; height 19 1/2" (49.5 cm), width 14 1/2" (37 cm).

LILITH: THE BURNEY PLAQUE

The Burney Plaque *(late Sumerian art—2300 B.C.E.)* of the winged Goddess, Lilith, a bird woman, has her flanked by sacred owls and she stands naked except for a tiara of horns, worn by all great deities. She holds the ring and rod of power. Her bird-taloned feet grip the backs of the reclining lions on which she stands *(power symbol)*. The owls reinforce the Goddess's nocturnal character. In Hebrew, Lilith's name means "screech owl" and she became a demon in Jewish folklore.

The dethroning of Lilith is recounted on cuneiform tablets. This poem is a parable of a much earlier Goddess and is similar to poems on Medusa, Inanna and her lover Gilgamesh, etc.

Lilith is a deity far older than Inanna. Owl-like, she builds her house in a tree. Lilith's lack of clothing creates an identification with the Naked Goddess, suggesting a state of nature. However powerful she may have been in early Sumerian times, she becomes a she-demon and temptress in the Old Testament.

In the Talmudic texts of the Kabbalistic period *(4th century C.E.)*, Lilith becomes an enchanting, seductive, destructive demon. The Talmud says that Lilith was formed by the Lord in response to Adam's request for a mate. In time, Lilith refused to lie submissively beneath Adam as he desired, and when he attempted force, she abandoned him.

At Adam's request, God sent angels to bring her back. They found her living with evil spirits near the Red Sea, where each day she gave birth to more than a hundred demons. She refused to return to Adam, although the angels told her that she would die if she did not submit. She reasoned that it was not possible for her to die since she had charge of all newborn infants. So God punished her by killing one hundred of her children each day.

Rafael Patai (*The Hebrew Goddess*) claims that Lilith went on to become the bride of Yahweh. Subsequently, Lilith was reduced to a succubus, seducing men who slept alone and killing newborns. The slander of the patriarchal scribes failed, however, and Lilith remained a powerful goddess in the Jewish folklore of central Europe up to the 16th Century.

Lady of the Beasts
Ancient Images of the Goddess and Her Sacred Animals (pp. 82-83)
Buffie Johnson
Harper & Row, San Francisco
1981

LILITH

Lilith is a Middle Eastern goddess of abundance, fertility and fecundity, the giver of agriculture to humans. The first woman created and the first wife of Adam, she refused to be subordinate to Adam in any way. Lilith is associated with the owl, a figure of darkness and deep wisdom, for she is also a goddess of death and transformation. She is sometimes represented as a demonic figure, for her dark wisdom and her sexual energy can be very threatening. She is known to appear as a frightening figure in dreams. Lilith is associated with the lotus, and the symbolism of that flower tells us much about her. The lotus, an exquisite flower that grows out of dark, rank, decaying earth, represents spiritual unfolding and the blossoming of the heart of wisdom. Like the lotus, Lilith challenges us to look upon our dark side and incorporate it into our wholeness so that our great beauty can blossom forth.

Boulet, Susan Seddon, The Goddess Paintings, text by Michael Babcock, Pomegranate Artbooks, San Francisco, 1994.

LILITH

Lilith, Angel of the Night, is a formidable and fearless Goddess. She is known in the Hebrew tradition as Adam's first wife. She left him, refusing to be subservient to him, and returned to her people of the Red Sea *(Egypt)*, a metaphor for her reunion with the moon-worshipping cultures who honored the female blood/menstrual mysteries. She became known as the Night Owl and a Dark Goddess.

I think of winged Lilith as a strong role model for women today who need encouragement to leave unhealthy relationships.

—Amulets of the Goddess,
Oracle of Ancient Wisdom
Nancy Blair *(Wingbow Press)*
Oakland, CA 1993, *p. 11.*

52

LILITH

Women are told *"give yourself,
submit yourself, Eve was created
as a helpmate for Adam, and you
should really live through taking
care of your husband and children."
It's a culture call to sacrifice, a
message intended only for women.*

See: **Sunday School Manifesto**
*Elizabeth Dodson Gray
Roundtable Press, Four Linden Square
Wellesley, Mass. 02181*

53

THE GENESIS STORY

Nowhere is the vigorous determination of patriarchy to suppress memories of the Primordial Mother more evident than in the Biblical Garden of Eden.

The Genesis story is a patriarchal revision of earlier Middle Eastern creation myths, and also of Hebrew tradition itself.

According to that tradition, as recorded in the Talmud, Adam's first wife was Lilith. Yahweh (or was it Elphim, that curious God-name which is feminine with a masculine plural ending?) created them both at the same time. But Lilith refused to subordinate herself to Adam, or to the male God - even physically: when Adam insisted that she must always lie beneath him during intercourse, she quarreled with him, flew up into the air and vanished. Adam appealed to Yahweh to bring her back, and Yahweh sent the three angels Senoi, Sansenoi and Samangloph to find her.

—The Witches Goddess
Janet & Stewart Farrar
Phoenix Publishing Company

LILITH IN THE BIBLE

In many translations the word Lilith is translated as "screech owl," "night hag," "night jar," or "night demon." The New Revised Standard Version and the Jerusalem Bible do not mention Lilith. The one single reference that survives is a statement about the threatened destruction of the nation of Edom.

> *Wild cats will meet hyenas there,*
> *The satyrs will call to each other,*
> *There Lilith shall repose*
> *and find her a place of rest.*
>
> *Isaiah 34:14*

Another translation reads:

Wildcats shall meet with hyenas, goat-demons shall call
  to each other;
  there too **Lilith** shall repose,
  and find a place to rest.
There shall they nest and lay and hatch
  and brood in its shadow;
  there too the buzzards shall gather,
  each one with its mate.

Isaiah 34:14-15 (New Revised Version)

Lily, the flower of Lilith

*("lilu" or lotus of the genital magic
in Sumero-Babylonian times)*

The lily was associated with virgin motherhood and carried over to Christian times by representing the flower that the angel Gabriel's hand used to filter God's semen, which entered Mary through her ear.* Paul warned women to cover their heads—since both angels and demons were believed to enter women through the ears.

The belief one could get pregnant via the ear resulted in the custom of women being required to cover their head/ears while in church.

Virgin births were popular for thousands of years among Egyptians, Chinese, Aztecs....

In 656, the 10th Council of Toledo adopted the holy day of Juno's miraculous conception of Mars into a commemoration of Mary's pregnancy via a lily.

* Walker, Barbara G., *The Woman's Encyclopedia of Myths and Secrets* (Harper & Row, San Francisco, 1983) p. 543.

DOCTRINE OF ORIGINAL SIN

....Original Sin was the primary ammunition used to subjugate women to the authority of Church, state and men. The idea of Original Sin was an unusual interpretation of creation myths that predate the composition of the book of Genesis by at least seven thousand years, starting in those lands in the Near East that were invaded by Jewish tribes. Here one finds symbols of the mythic garden of life: the serpent representing rebirth, the "world tree," the "sun eternal," and "ever-living waters." There is no wrath, no evil, no guilt or unpleasantness associated with the garden.

In the Judeo-Christian myth, the serpent (no longer a symbol of wisdom and rebirth), tempts woman "to eat of the fruit of the tree" (which no longer represents wisdom, but rather an act of disobedience to the one god). And woman, likewise, tempts her mate. Her punishment is to forever bring forth children in pain, and to be subservient to man. The pleasures of living in a paradise on earth give way to shame over nakedness, conception, birth, indeed life itself.

The dogma of the 13th century drew on the philosophy of St. Augustine, who held that only the Church could absolve one of this sin. It was an ingenious play of power that kept people chained to the institution with guarantees of forgiveness and eternal life.

Women lost on all counts.

—Woman As Healer
Jeanne Achterberg
Shambhala, Boston (1991)
pp. 66-67.

The story of Lilith is important because it illustrates the suppression of women and female sexuality. The story of Lilith illustrates the transition between ancient female Goddess worship and the later one-male-God worship.

Lilith: Near East; Sumerian

Weather; Disorder; Evil; Moon and Night; Education and Knowledge; Justice.

Lilith is one of many names given to the Great Mother Goddess who represented the earth, the universe, life and death; the seasons, and the wind. Later, Lilith became an early Sumerian storm demon *(Lilitu)* mentioned in a text dated *ca* 2400 B.C.E. In Hebrew scriptures, Isaiah called her a night monster who haunts Edom. The Talmud describes her as a "charming woman." In <u>The Alphabet of Ben Sira</u> *(11th century)* the first people were Adam and Lilith; Lilith taught Adam wisdom. According to rabbinical legend, Lilith is Adam's first wife who flew away. To the Arabs, Lilith is "The Holy Lady."

In feminist thealogy, Lilith's story is expanded:

—In the beginning, God formed Adam and Lilith from dust and made them equal. Adam tried to order Lilith about and she grew very tired of this attempt to control her, invoked the name of God, and flew out of the Garden. God then created Eve for Adam, and for awhile she existed as his subordinate helpmate.

Adam told Eve about the horrible demon, Lilith, who lived on the other side of the wall. One day, Eve climbed the wall and happened upon Lilith. Though she was frightened, Eve did not run, but stayed and talked with her. They told each other stories and taught each other many things, and a bond of Sisterhood grew between them. God and Adam were apprehensive, fearing the power of this new alliance. Today, males continue to fear women who organize for social change.

59

WE ARE SISTERS ON A JOURNEY

We are sisters on a journey
Shining in the sun.
Shining through the darkest night
The healing has begun *(repeat line)*.

We are sisters on a journey
Singing now as one.
Remembering the ancient ones
The women and the wisdom *(repeat line)*.

LILITH BIBLIOGRAPHY

Aristophanes, *The Frogs* in Hutchins, Robert Maynard GREAT BOOKS OF THE WESTERN WORLD: AESCHYLUS, SOPHOCLES, EURIPIDES, ARISTOPHANES (Chicago: Encyclopaedia Britannica, Inc.,1952), p. 567 (re Empusa, as monster, in lines 277-314).

Armstrong, Karen, *A History of God: The 4,000-Year Quest of Judaism, Christianity, and Islam* (Alfred Knopf, NY, 1993).

Austen, Hallie Inglehart, *The Heart of the Goddess: Art, Myth and Meditations of the World's Sacred Feminine* (Berkeley: Wingbow Press, 1990), p. 128-129. Includes large photo of ancient plaque of Lilith.

Begg, Ean, *The Cult of the Black Virgin* (London: Arkana/Routledge & Kegan Paul, 1985).

Bible (two translations in which **Lilith** is used in **Isaiah 34:14** instead of "screech owl" or "night hag", etc.).

* *Jerusalem Bible, The* (NY; Oxford Univ. Press, 1991), p. 1020.
* *The New Oxford Annotated Bible* (NY: Oxford Univ. Press, 1991) p. 911.

Blair, Nancy, *Amulets of the Goddess, Oracle of Ancient Wisdom* (Wingbow Press, Oakland, CA, 1993), p. 11.

Borges, Jorge Luis, *The Book of Imaginary Beings* (NY: Discus Books/ Avon, 1969), p. 149.

DeMontalvo, Soledad, *Women, Food and Sex In History,Vol. I (4-volume set from* American Atheist Press, Austin, Tx, 1988).

Durdin-Robertson, *The Goddesses of Chaldea, Syria and Egypt,* Cesar Publications, Huntington Castle, Clonegal, Enniscarthy, Eire, MMMMCCCXXIII pp. 220-221; 234-235.

Eliade, Mircea, *The Encylopedia of Religion* (NY: Macmillan, 1987), pp. 554-555 of Vol. 8.

Encyclopedia Judaica (Jerusalem: Macmillan Co., 1971), pp. 245-249 of Vol. 11.

Farrar, Janet & Stewart, *The Witches Goddess* (Phoenix Pub. Co., Portal Way, Box 10, Custer, WA 98240), pp. 130-131.

Fontenrose, Joseph, *PYTHON: A Study of Delphic Myth and Its Origins* (Berkeley: Univ. of Calif. Press, 1959-80) p. 172.

Gadon, Elinor, *The Once and Future Goddess: A Symbol for Our Time* (San Francisco: Harper, 1989), pp. 122, 123-125.

Gimbutas, Marija, *The Language of the Goddess* (San Francisco: Harper & Row, 1989), p. 190.

Goethe, Johann Wolfwang von, *Gaust:Sc.21,Walpurgisnacht* (Bayard Taylor, tr.).

Goldenberg, Judith Plascow w/Karen Bloomquist, Margaret Early, and Elizabeth Farians, *Religion and Sexism: Images of Woman in the Jewish and Christian Traditions (NY: Simon & Shuster), 1974) Epilogue pp. 341-343.*

Graves, Robert, *The White Goddess: A Historical Grammar of Poetic Myth* (NY: Farrar, Straus & Giroux, 1948/80), p. 220, 315.

Graves, Robert, *The Greek Myths* (in 2 vols.) (Middlesex, England: Penguin Books, 1955/60), Vol. I, pp. 189-190.

Graves, Robert & Raphael Patai, *Hebrew Myths: The Book of Genesis* (NY: Greenwich House, 1963/83), pp. 65-69.

Headley, Mary K., *The Great Goddess, Our Many Names* (137 31st St., Boulder, CO 80303-3401, 1993), p. 54.

Johnson, Buffie *Lady of the Beasts: Ancient Images of the Goddess and Her Sacred Animals* (San Francisco: Harper & Row, 1988), pp. 82-83. *(Includes line drawing of plaque.)*

Josephson, Shirley Trout, poem: *"Pruning From The Garden of Eden"* The Communicator of UUWF: April/May 1990, p. 8.

Koltuv, Barbara Black, *The Book of Lilith* (York Beach, Maine: Nicolas-Hays, Inc., 1986). *(Includes Lilith bibliography.)*

Kramer, Samuel Noah, *The Sumerians: Their History, Culture and Character* (Chicago: Univ. of Chicago Press, 1963) pp. 198, 200, 202, 258.

Leach, Maria, ed., *Funk & Wagnalls Standard Dictionary of Folklore, Mythology, and Legend* (San Francisco: Harper & Row), pp. 622-623.

Monaghan, Patricia, *The Book of Goddesses and Heroines* (NY: E.P. Dutton, 1981) pp. 179-180.

MacCullough, John, ed., *Mythology of All Races*, (13 vols.) (Boston: Archaeological Institute of America, Marshall Jones Co., 1932), II-224; V-353, 361, 362, 363, 365; VII-88.

Neumann, Erich, *The Great Mother: An Analysis of the Archetype* (Princeton Univ. Press: 1955/91), p. 81. *(146n, Plate 126.)*

Noble, Vicki, *Motherpeace: A Way to the Goddess Through Myth, Art, and Tarot* (San Francisco: Harper & Row, 1983) p. 55,86, 130, 131 Lilith (Moon Goddess).

Pagels, Elaine, *Adam, Eve, and the Serpent* (NY: Random House, 1988).

Parker, Derek & Julia, *The Immortals: The Mysterious World of Gods, Goblins, Fairies, Leprechauns, Vampires, Witches, and Devils* (San Francisco: McGraw Hill, 1976), p. 21.

Patai, Raphael, *The Hebrew Goddess* (NY: Discus/Avon, 1967/78).

Phillips, J.A., *The History of An Idea* (San Francisco: Harper & Row, 1984).

Pirani, Alix, *The Absent Mother: Restoring the Goddess to Judaism and Christianity* (London: Mandala, 1991).

Pritchard, James B., *Ancient Near Eastern Texts: Relating to the Old Testament* (3rd edition, with Supplement) (Princeton, NY: Princeton Univ. Press, 1969) , p. 658.

Rossetti, Daniel Gabriel: (two poems):

* *"Lilith"*, Sonnet LXXVII in *Body's Beauty* Doughty, Oswald, ed., *Rosetti's Poems* (London: Everyman's Library #627. NY: E.P. Dutton & Co., 1912/61),p 142.

* *"Eden Bower"* in *The Poems of Dante Gabriel Rossetti*: Vol. I of II). See *The Blessed Damozel and Longer Poems* (Troy, NY: Pafraets Book Co., 1903), pp. 215-222.

Ruether, Rosemary Radford, *Womanguides*; *Readings Toward a Feminist Theology* (Boston: Beacon Press, 1985).

Saggs, H.W.F., *The Greatness That Was Babylon: A Survey of the Ancient Civilization of the Tigris-Euphrates Valley* (NY: Hawthorn Books, 1962) p. 309, 485.

Sjoo, Monica & Barbara Mor, *The Great Cosmic Mother: Rediscovering the Religion of the Earth* (San Francisco: Harper & Row, 1987) pp. 276-277.

Stone, Merlin, *Ancient Mirrors of Womanhood: Our Goddess and Heroine Heritage* (NY: New Sibylline Books, 1979; this edition is published in two volumes) Vol. I, pp. 127-128.

Stone, Merlin, *When God Was A Woman* (NY: Harvest/Harcourt Brace Jovanovich, 1976), pp. 158-159, 195.

Walker, Barbara G., *The Woman's Encyclopedia of Myths and Secrets* (San Francisco: Harper & Row, 1983), pp. 541-542;543; 106-109;290;903-909.

Waterman, Philip F. *The Story of Superstition* (NY: Alfred A. Knopf, 1929), p. 75 *(uses ineffable name)*; 278-284 *(one full chapter, "The Legend of Lilith")*.

Wittig, *Les Guerilleres* (NY: Bard Book/Avon, 1963/73), p. 89. Beacon Press has a 1985 edition.

Wolkstein, Diane and Samuel Noah Kramer, *Inanna: Queen of Heaven and Earth: Her Stories and Hymns from Sumer* (NY: Harper & Row, 1983), pp. 5-6 and 51 (illus.); 141-142;160, 179, 189.

Womanspirit (magazine):

(1) Terra, *Lilith* (poem) Winter, 1974, p. 35;

(2) Anderson, Katherine, *The Second Time Around* (poem) Summer, 1980, *p. 29.*

PRUNINGS FROM THE GARDEN OF EDEN

I

I wince
to hear the honeysuckle scream,
until I hear the thorny quince
breathe "ahhhh..."

II

God made Adam and Eve, it's said,
and set them in the Garden of Eden
to tend and prune it.
Did you ever attempt to tend an orchard?

Eve talked Adam
into tasting the fruit
and suddenly they could see
everything.

God banished them
to a stony land
where living depends
upon the sweat of one's brow.

Call it sour figs
if you like
but I've been thinking
perhaps not enough
is better
than too much.

III

Adam and Eve?
Unbelievable.
Adam was a poor creature.
Obedient, trusting Adam
didn't think to question
what he's told.
But he'd never make a Marine.
Couldn't take the blame.
And Eve?
Adam called her
Mother-of-all-living.
Innocent, open-minded,
curious Eve.
Logical, testing,
imaginative Eve.
Such a one
could seduce
a wise old serpent.

What about that serpent?
The beguiling
serpent.
The only one who didn't lie.
It was an awful crime
and the serpent took the blame
but they never did find the motive.
Perhaps she couldn't believe in a god
who'd put himself
above the truth.

God?
God the All-powerful.
God the Father.
With Eve the Mother?
An unstable combination
bound to end sometime
in someone's
crucifixion.

Loyal, loving Eve
took the punishment,
went with Adam
and made babies
for God.

Next time around
she ought to choose
the serpent.

--Shirley Trout Josephson
Hatboro, Pennsylvania

TOWARD A DEFINITION OF
FEMINIST SPIRITUALITY

A belief system emphasizing the female aspect in our quest for personal and global wholeness and harmony. In attitude, there is respect for all interconnectedness of nature and all its cycles and for all stages of life; empowerment and freedom of belief for ourselves and others; body-mind-spirit inclusiveness, rather than exclusiveness; community rather than hierarchy; and, the pluralistic nature of truth. Practices and rituals may draw from ancient religions, current religions, and rituals created by and for ourselves. Among the many symbols and objects revered are: the circle, the moon, the earth and the sea.

Our words are designed especially for women, but they may also include men. After all, both women and men may be feminists.

Feminist Spirituality challenges and reclaims traditional assumptions, affirms life, respects nature, cherishes age, encourages people to be stewards of our planet rather than exploiters, and reclaims words such as goddess, crone, pagan, witch....

Feminist Spirituality embraces reverence for nurturing, love, connection with the remote past, community, holism, intimacy, inclusivity, the moon and the dark.

Feminist Spirituality values freedom, choice, empowerment, personal responsibility, circles, unity, changing perceptions, searching, intuition, peace, healing, and laughter.

--from *Mary F. Heath*
Women & Religion Task Force
Pacific Central District
Unitarian Universalist Association
March 14, 1985

ISHTAR

Perhaps her rage was too intense,
Her passion too demanding,
Her love too inclusive,
Her followers too many.
She had to be stopped.

Stopped by a dreary old man god,
Who codified all of life
On stone tablets, like grave markers;
A petty, vengeful god
Who requires the sacrifice of children.

You men are the losers:
Now you'll never see us
Bare armed, dancing, our hair
Gleaming in the sunshine;
Pleasuring ourselves - and you.

You've imprisoned us in house and tent,
You fear us and call us unclean
When our moon flux is upon us.
We can only chart the goddess' course
Across the sky - and within us.

And wait and pray that her memory
Will rise again in women's dreams,
And that one day women will pour the wine
And bake her cakes
And revel in her light and love.

Written by Helen Szymkowiak
*during a **Cakes For the Queen***
*of **Heaven** class at First Unitarian*
Church, Baltimore, MD.

The treasury at Delphi, Greece.

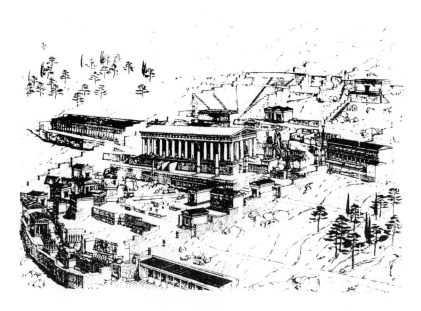

Delphi

A 10-MINUTE HISTORY OF PATRIARCHY

Meg Bowman

Throughout most of human history, people generally co-operated with one another. For tens of thousands of years, our ancestors lived in small groups and worshipped *(valued/ gave worth to)* the female/feminine/ fertility. It was magic when a woman *(or a cow, ibex, goat, ewe....)* gave birth. It was magic when the dark winter gave way to spring and flowers bloomed and wild grains, vegetables and fruit grew.

HUNTING BEGINS

About 40,000 years ago, our ancestors learned that putting sharpened ends of long sticks into a fire hardened them into spears. Many men with narrow hips *(good for running and chasing)* and strong pectoral muscles *(good for throwing)* became hunters. Many women, wide of hip and often pregnant or nursing a baby, stayed close to the cave or shelter *(usually near a river or lake)* where they gathered wild roots, grains, and other food staples. The first 'families' were women and their children — the role of sperm in reproduction was unknown.

71

DOMESTICATION OF ANIMALS/AGRICULTURE

Throughout most of human history, our ancestors were itinerant scavengers/gatherers/nomads. Until the domestication of animals *(dogs, goats, sheep, pigs, cattle, camels...)* and the development of crude agriculture, there were few people on our planet. Then, about 10,000 year ago, some of our ancestors learned agriculture— the magic of planting seeds and seeing them grow. Settled communities evolved and, with a relatively secure food supply, populations expanded. With the domestication of animals, our ancestors also learned the connection of sex to reproduction. The female did not magically reproduce, she needed male seed. The woman needed a man; the cow needed the bull. Men began to worship bulls.

> Learning that sperm played a part in reproduction is the most significant social change in human history. This knowledge triggered a change from matrilineal/goddess/fertility/female-centered cooperative societies to patrilineal/ gods/patriarchal/male-centered competitive social paradigms with men exercising **power over** women, children, animals, and Mother Nature.

Men began to worship the phallus *(phallicism)*, erecting huge phalluses and later, in Greece, wearing an apron with an attached erect cloth penis. In Rome, on the Ides of March, phallic statues were paraded in the streets. The May Pole, flag poles and obelisks are all phallic symbols.

Some men, now living in settled communities and accustomed to hunting and herding animals, came up with the idea of owning property and proclaimed **my** goats, **my** pigs, **my** water well....

The idea of private property was enforced by those men who took power as kings/obas/pharaohs/emperors/ patriarchs... Women no longer owned their homes. Men declared themselves heads of households; a man's home was **his** castle and don't forget it! It was important that he have sons to inherit that castle, **his** name, **his** crown, **his** "blood" *(genes)*, **his** animals, **his** land.... Matrilineal societies *(ancestry traced through the mother)* became patrilineal *(ancestry traced through forefathers)*. Remember the biblical Abraham/Issac/ etc. who begat? Men begat, women did not bear.

MOTHERHOOD: A MATTER OF FACT
FATHERHOOD: A MATTER OF CONJECTURE

The idea of "marriage" *(to wed)* was created to ensure the patriarch "legal" heirs to inherit **his** property *(land, camels, goats, whatever)* and **his** name/title/ "royal blood"/whatever. Upper-class marriages were carefully arranged to join two families for the purpose of increasing patriarchal political and economic power.

Patriarchs went to great lengths to assure the virginity of their daughters, and to be sure that it was only their seed planted in their legal wife — the female oven or incubator. The belief that **he** planted a complete human being into the female incubator continued until the 17th century and the invention of the microscope *(yes, even Aristotle believed this)*. Women became domestic chattel and forced marriages/battery/incest/rape/molest/harassment.... became a woman's lot.

Women had few, if any, options; their role was to produce sons. The word family *(familia)* originally meant 'a man and his slaves'. Patriarchs had **absolute power-over** their wives *(concubines/harem/mistresses)* and children. Rich men **ruled over** their family, clan, tribe, fiefdom, city-state, kingdom, empire; slaves, serfs, servants, peasants and commoners. Patriarchs decided who would marry whom, who would live or die, and who he would sell, beat, or impregnate.

Proof of virginity before marriage was demanded*
and wide-spread female genital mutilation *(excision of the*

---

* *In Europe eunuchs were employed in palaces as chamberlains. For centuries, people were employed to "watch" the queen sleep to be sure that **only** the royal seed was planted. The cult of virginity also emerged to ensure that no seed had reached the bride before the marriage (e.g. Lady Diane had to have two doctors certify her virginity before marrying into the British Royal family).*

clitoris and/or infibulation, sewing up the vagina *) became mandatory. Traditions evolved and men passed thousands of laws to control women's bodies and deny women basic civil and human rights.

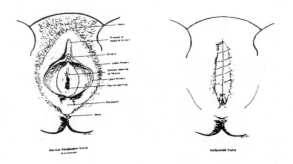

Normal Adolescent Vulva

Infibulated Vulva

* **excision:** *surgically remove all or part of the clitoris by knife, razor blade, scissors, etc.*
infibulation: cut off labia major and minora, then sew up the vagina, leaving a tiny opening for urine and menses. This mutilation often results in shock and infections, plus health problems resulting from retained urine and blood. During childbirth, a woman is disinfibulated (cut open), then sewn back up again. FGM (sometimes called 'female circumcision'— a misnomer) is painful and detrimental to a woman's health.

FGM has been practiced for several thousand years. It is part of the patriarchal pattern of **power over** *women. Today, in over 38 countries, over 128 million girls have been vaginally mutilated. Female genital mutilation goes back to the dawn of patriarchy. Excision and infibulation are used not only to curtail female sexuality, but as a pattern of patriarchy used to subordinate/exploit/control women. FGM is violence against females, and, along with rape, incest, molest, harassment, battery... reflects patriarchy, the oldest of injustices.*

75

As men took power, they began to distrust women. After all, a daughter might run away and elope, a wife might have an affair and get pregnant by a man who is not her husband, she might desert a husband, or protest being a wife, a brood mare, a drudge, a chattel, a servant to men....

To ensure that only **his** seed was planted into **his** legal wife *(or wives),* the patriarch created segregated quarters (*e.g. purdah)* guarded by castrated males *(eunucks*).* **His** women were required to wear veils *(e.g. shador)* and the sexual double standard reigned supreme. **He** had a harem, seraglio, concubines, mistresses and then created the idea of an "illegitimate child," one who could **not** inherit **his** property or **his** name. Chaperones were required to guarantee a daughter's virginity, but you just can't trust females so FGM *(female genital mutilation—clitoridectomies, excisions, infibulations)* became the norm throughout many lands. Millions upon millions of females were mutilated; after all, a wife was to produce sons, **not** enjoy sex.

Later, during the Crusades, European men forced women into torturous leather and metal chastity belts. During the Victorian era, tightly corseted women, unable to breath, suffered from the vapors. For over 800 years, upper-class Chinese men had a foot fetish so that females had their feet bound in order to attract a husband *(her only option was marriage or being sold into concubinage or slavery).*

---

* *On the island of Zanzibar, thousands of boys were castrated to guard harems. The Catholic church castrated boys in order for them to maintain their soprano voices. Today, there are about 400,000 castrated males in India, many of whom are prostitutes.*

The sexual double-standard became universal. Until 1977 a man could sue for divorce on the grounds of adultery in Minnesota, but a wife could not sue her husband for divorce on the grounds of adultery. Today, there are areas of the world where an adulterous woman *(or a pregnant unmarried girl)* is still stoned to death and a woman needs several male witnesses to prove rape; in Pakistan, a married woman who accuses a man of rape can be imprisoned on the charge of adultery. In Brazil, a woman who disobeys her husband can be killed and the husband will **not** be prosecuted— he was upholding **his** honor. Several societies still require virginity verified before marriage and in Iran and Algeria, women must wear veils or risk having acid or feces thrown in their face. Women are still sequestered in segregated quarters in Morocco. Thousands of laws/practices/ traditions designed to control women's sexuality/bodies/behavior remain in effect today—it's called **patriarchy**.

SKY GODS AND WARS

It wasn't long before men began to fight over **their** property, **their** power, **their** male gods *(Zeus/Osiris, Horus, Thor, Yahweh/Allah ...)*. Armies were organized and wars, many wars, were fought. Women became the spoils of war, the enemy's property to rape and abuse, and, yes, even today suffer, along with children, from bombings and other horrors wars inflict upon civilian populations.

Wars in Europe began between 3,000 and 2,100 B.C.E. *(Before the Common Era)*, except on the Greek island of Crete where women continued to hold power long after men in other parts of the world had ''taken over'.

Strong macho sky gods were created about the same time men started killing each other in disputes over who owned what. Male-run religions with their phallic worship and male god(s) deliberately destroyed female-centered temples and goddess worship; earth-honoring goddesses were brutally destroyed or co-opted as women became the property of men. Example: For thousands of years, people had sought justice and advice from the Oracle at Delphi *(temples located on beautiful mountain slopes northwest of Athens, Greece named for the goddess Athena)*. People came by ship and by foot to gain wisdom and guidance from the Priestess, representing Gaea, the Great Mother of the Universe. When priests took over, using a drugged woman as a front, Delphi became a male hive of activity dedicated to patriarchal values and male gods. Greek plays went so far as to proclaim that women were not even parents. Orestes said, "No mother gave me birth." *

NEW MYTHS

Even though the goddess Athena had been worshipped for thousands of years, Greeks were told that Athena had been born from Zeus' forehead! Athena, goddess of wisdom and love, became the goddess of war — with a spear and a helmet.

Goddess temples and goddess worshippers were brutally destroyed. Some women who protested against patriarchy and its Sky God(s) were called Amazons or witches

* *"The mother is not the parent of the child, only the nurse....*
  The parent is the father who commits His seed to her...."

and killed. Ruling men took over all religious, political, educational, economic and medical institutions. Women were declared inferior to men and non-persons *(certainly non-citizens when nation states emerged)*. English Common Law *(transported to America)* decreed that a married woman had **no** rights.

Denied freedom and choices, women internalized patriarchal values, including a male Sky God. Sally Kempton noted, *"It is hard to fight an enemy who has outposts in your head."*

Today, studies of ancient Delphi and Crete *(Greece)*, Catul Huyuk and Ephesus *(now in Turkey)*, BoPan *(near Xi'an, China)*.... reveal a time when women were held in high esteem, a time when women owned their homes and their bodies, a time when people cooperated with one another, a time before patriarchy and its jealous Sky God and many wars.

Tholos 4th c. BCE
Delphi

Temple of Apollo
330 BCE Delphi

80

ST. PATRICK'S DAY: MARCH 17

"St. Patrick is special to the Irish because he brought us Christianity when we were still being lied to by the Druids, and he drove out all the snakes from Ireland to make it like the Garden of Eden without the serpent."

—Scarlett, Alexandra Ripley, *p. 466*
*(sequel to **Gone With the Wind**)*

The story of a St. Patrick driving all the snakes out of Ireland is a myth. The snake symbolized old Goddess religions. During the centuries when Christianity was being brutally forced upon the Druids, Ireland was **not** infested with snakes.*   Early Christians killed **people** who practiced the old female/fertility/earth-based/ Goddess-centered religion, **not** snakes.

* There were no snakes in Ireland. During the last Ice Age, when most of Britain was under ice, the climate was too cold for reptiles until less than 10,000 years ago. Most of the English Channel was dry land at that time, and reptiles that could withstand the cold could have migrated into southern England. As the climate grew warm enough for snakes, ice melted, waters rose and for a period of less than 1,000 years there may have been a land link to Ireland and a climate in which the hardiest reptiles could survive, but the snake arrived too late and only the common lizard made the crossing. The St. Patrick legend is a myth.

<u>*Snakes of the World*</u>
Hampton Wildman Parker

81

There may have been an Irish knight Sir Patrice, but St. Patrick is a fictitious figure built on Roman **pater** or **patricius**, a priest. St. Patrick's Day was known throughout the Roman Empire as a March 17th *(Ides of March)* festival when a giant phallus was paraded through the streets and solemnly crowned with a garland representing the divine yoni *(the genital focus of the Goddess' reproductive energy)* by the hands of a specially selected matron. *

The only evidence of a Christian St. Patrick is an autobiography supposedly written in the 5th century, but not heard of until 400 years later. It was forged by monks wishing to pretend that the Irish were converted as early as the 5th century *(Christianity had failed to take root as late as the 12th* century!).

* *Barbara G. Walker, **The Woman's Encyclopedia of Myths and Secrets** (Harper & Row, 1983), pp. 774-775.*

NOTE: Phallic worship was a focal point under ancient patriarchal Greek and Roman cultures and in European festivals, such as May Day when the May Pole, representing the penis, was stuck into Mother Earth *(to assure bountiful crops)* and then decorated by dancing virgins. To assure fertile fields, a nobleman would have sex with the Queen of the May *(usually an attractive serf or peasant girl)* on newly ploughed land. To be selected Queen of the May was a great honor. As a child, besides decorating the May Pole, we exchanged May Baskets on May 1st. When an adolescent, my mother sometimes asked me, "Who do you think you are, Queen of the May?"

May Day

May Day *(May 1st)* has been celebrated for centuries as **Beltane**, or the half year. It is now six months since Samhain *(Halloween)* which started the New Year for many of our European ancestors.

Beltane was the great Springtime festival of the European witches. In Ireland and Scotland, the time was celebrated with the god Baal, Bel, or Balder* burned in effigy. Today, in rural Scandinavia, fires on **Beltane** are still called "Balder's balefires." ** Today, great bonfires are lit throughout Norway as people party through the night.***

During Medieval times, the May King won the "Queen of the Magic Wood" *(the Goddess)* by combat with her previous king. The new king became the ritual lover of the Queen and led the sexual games of May Day. Yes, May Day is an ancient fertility holiday which was celebrated with great sexual license and freedom.

The May Pole represented the god's phallus planted in the earth's womb. This phallic symbol, bedecked with pastel ribbons, was then danced around by young, virgin girls celebrating Spring, fertility, the new crops.

The custom probably originated in India as a celebration of the Goddess Kali and was a time of not only sexual license, but women talked back to men; servants and slaves talked back to their master and mistress; and everyone drank and danced and feasted and frolicked. Marriage vows were temporarily in abeyance.

---

* *Son of Odin and Frigga and god of light and peace in Norse mythology.*
** *Origin of balderdash (17th c. 'an odd mixture')?*
*** *It has often been stated, "Scratch a Scandinavian and you get a Pagan."*

One Indian writer described the holiday thusly:

"Young men and maids, old men and wives, run overnight to the woods, groves, hills, and mountains, where they spend all night in pleasant pastimes, and in the morning they return, bringing with them birch and branches of trees, to decorate their homes. One was named as a great Lord, as superintendent over their pastimes and sports. And they also bring home a May-pole, in great veneration. They have twenty or forty yoke of oxen, every ox having a sweet nosegay of flowers placed on the tips of his horns. The May-pole is covered all over with flowers and herbs, bound round with strings, from top to bottom and sometimes painted with various colors. Two or three hundred men, women and children follow it with great devotion. They set up the pole in a place where arbors and bowers are close by. They dance around it." *

In medieval European times, knights and ladies rode in pairs into the woods, led by the Queen of the May on a white horse and her male companion on a dark one. They impersonated Frey and Freya, the Lord and Lady whose union made fertility magic each Spring.

The Holy Roman Empire—the Catholic church— was opposed to this ancient religious festival and declared May to be dedicated to Mary, but that didn't stop the people who knew that it really belonged to Maya or Maia, the Virgin Goddess of Spring.

* *See: Walker, Barbara G., The Woman's Encyclopedia of Myths and Secrets, pp. 624-626.*

May was the traditional month of "the wearing of the green" in honor of the Earth Mother's new garment, and of fornicating in newly plowed fields to encourage bountiful crops. May was the time of sexual freedom throughout rural Europe. "Spring was in the air...."

Have you ever heard that "only bad women marry in the month of May?" This is probably a relic of earlier taboos on all marriages during this month of sexual license.

When I was a child growing up in North Dakota, we had May-pole dances with young girls *(virgins)* weaving the pastel colored ribbons around the May-pole. We celebrated friendships by making May Baskets out of colored construction paper, filling them with wild flowers and candies and then taking them to a friend or neighbor's house where we would knock on their door and quickly run away. That was how they knew that someone liked them.

Today, May Day is celebrated in some Eastern European cities with parades and a day off from work. Sometimes there are flowers and dancing, but mostly it's a commemoration of International Worker's Day.

MOON GODDESS

A Reading For 13 Female Voices

Directions:

Photocopy "Moon Goddess" and then cut the script into the 13 speaking parts. Give each of the 13 women readers a numbered part to read for the moon ritual. Under a full moon, participants stand in a circle. The facilitator can introduce the ritual by saying, *"In some ways, the moon has traditionally been thought of in negative ways. Think of the words 'lunatic' and 'lunacy'. All they really mean is 'affected by the moon'. Our ancient ancestors had great respect for the moon and tonight we will honor the Moon Goddess."*

Following the reading of these 13 parts, have participants sing a chant. Afterwards, ask each woman to speak what is in her heart.

This can be followed by a healing ritual, or a celebration, or a dance, or songs.... and can end with another chant.

Be sure there is enough light for reading *(perhaps each reader can hold a candle or a small flashlight.)*

MOON GODDESS
(for 13 female voices)

1. *(RAISE AND THEN LOWER ARMS TO MOON)*

Oh, lovely Moon Goddess,
  Bless us, your daughters,
As we raise our arms to you,
  The bright full moon.

2. *(RAISE AND THEN LOWER FACE TO MOON)*

Hear us now,
  As we raise our faces to yours.
Look behind our words
  For the feelings hidden from others
And sometimes
  Even from ourselves.

3.   Light our faces
         And a pathway for our journeys.
       Heal our bodies
         And our spirits.
       Add your radiance to our smiles.

       Love us, and help us find the way to peace,
         For our lives have just begun.

4.   Oh, lovely Moon Goddess,
            We hear the dark mysterious drums and
        We call you from within our souls:
            We call you from the depths
        Of our inner selves.

        We will now listen
            and hear what you have to say.

5.   *(PAUSE)*

        Moon Goddess,
            Let your midnight song
        Find us among our Sisters.
            Let the flute of the moonbeam
        Become the sound of all who call Earth home—
            As we heal ourselves
        And our beloved planet.

6.   Show us how we may better know you,
            Oh, lovely Moon Goddess.
        Moving constant in the skies
            Around the Earth, our Mother—
        Help us to know the ways of Nature
            And live in peace
        with all Earth's creatures.

7. Goodnight and good-bye,
        Man-in-the-Moon.
    You have overstayed your welcome.

        Welcome home, Moon Goddess,
    Known by many names.
    In the crescent moon
        And in the splendor of the full moon,
    You have always been with us.

8. Great Goddess Moon,
        Now we are one.
    Long have we suffered
        Without your Wisdom.

    We have awakened!
        We sing, dance and play,
    Filled with your presence.

9. Sky borne companion,
        In the darkness we speak to you.
    We speak of loves sought and gained,
      Of memories that mark the past,
      Of present hopes and dreams.
    All these,
    We share with you.

10.   Playing in the meadows,
           Driving on the freeways,
             Walking on the seashore,
      Flying in a jet plane,
           Climbing in the mountains,
      We ask, and you comfort us
           With your healing moonbeams.

11.   Great Goddess Moon,
           We are your daughters.
      We listen to the river
           And we hear the voices
             of our foremothers—
      Who call through time immemorial.

      Our Sisters, strong survivors,
           Call and strengthen us.

12.   Tonight, our Sisters smile
           With tearful eyes
      For though we may not meet again,
           We know
      All time is one—and
           We treasure this moment.

      We dance with the joy of being together—
           As we are one,
           Sisters of the Moon.

13.   Great Goddess Moon of Forever
            Who guards our sacred Earth—
       You keep us strong
            To meet the coming days and nights.

       Everyone, please repeat after me:

            We rejoice. *(ECHO)*
            Our power is one. *(ECHO)*
            Blessed Be. *(ECHO)*

Facilitator's Note:
At the end of the " Moon Goddess" reading, lead participants
in a chant, such as found on p. 60.
Then say: *"Tonight we call forth healing and love, strength
and understanding. This is a time for each of us to speak what
is in her heart; to be in touch with our feelings. Speak now:
Let us, your Sisters, hear the words so that we may know
what is in your heart."*

(ALLOW TIME FOR EACH WOMAN TO HAVE THE OPPORTUNITY TO SPEAK.)

"We will end our Moon Ritual by/with...." (healing ritual,
dance, chant, group hug.... whatever is apropos for your group).

—*Meg Bowman, with help from her friends
Joys Angels and Mary F. Heath.*
Inspired after reading *"Impressions of the Peyote Ritual,"*
L. Henson from Keepers of Arrows: Poems for the Cheyenne,
Renaissance Press, Chickasha, OH 1971.

CIRCLE OF SISTERHOOD

by

Dorothy Satir

This is a dramatic reading by five women.
The women stand apart, addressing the audience as each
speaks her lines. The others listen, look at each speaker
and murmur or nod in recognition at what she says.

At first, the women speak of their status as sisters or
nonsisters. Then the disappointments or hurts in sister-
hood are related.

Following, we hear of good sisterly remembrances,
in either past or present tense.

Finally, we learn how to gain a sister and be a sister,
and the audience is brought into the Circle of Sisterhood.

The chorus lines can be recited in a plaintive, longing
voice.

(CHORUS): I NEVER HAD A SISTER.
             WHAT'S IT LIKE? *(repeat both lines)*

(read slowly, sadly, plaintively)

READER #1: I once had a sister —
               now she is gone.

READER #2: I have a sister,
               but she lives far away.

READER #3: I was adopted.
I don't even know if I have a sister.

READER #4: I had a sister, but she died at birth.

READER #5: I have two sisters,
but we're all so busy.

READER #1: I had a brother, but no sister.

READER #2: I was an only child.

READER #3: My sister died before I was born.

(CHORUS)   I NEVER HAD A SISTER.
WHAT'S IT LIKE? *(repeat both lines)*

---

*Pause. Some women exchange places.
Allow time for the words to sink in.*

(read angrily, anguished, resigned; whatever emotion fits)

READER #1: I had a sister. She was mean to me.

READER #2: My sister is ten years older than I.

READER #3: I quarreled with my sister
and we never made up!

94

READER #4: I was a little sister; I hated that.

READER #5: My sister stole my boyfriend!

READER #1: My sister has been in an institution for years.

READER #2: I always had to wear my sister's
hand-me-downs.

(CHORUS) I NEVER HAD A SISTER.
WHAT'S IT LIKE? *(repeat both lines)*

READER #3: I lost my sister in an automobile accident.

READER #4: Mom liked my sister best.

READER #5: My sister died of cancer.

READER #1: My sister and I live nearby,
but we're so involved with our families.

READER #2: My sister and I grew apart when we
married and moved away.

READER #3: After my parents' divorce,
my sister and I hardly saw each other.

READER #4: My sister resented me because
I went to college and she didn't.

(CHORUS) I NEVER HAD A SISTER.
WHAT'S IT LIKE? *(repeat both lines)*

Pause and shift places, as before.

(read softly, clearly, warmly and with affection)

READER #1: I remember how my sister
always took care of me.

READER #2: My sister and I talk on the phone every week.

READER #3: My sister took the place of my mother
when my mother died.

READER #4: My sister and I fought a lot —
but we always made up.

READER #5: I always feel my sister's love around me.

READER #1: My sister taught me what Kotex was for.

(CHORUS) I WISH I HAD A SISTER! *(Repeat)*

READER #2: I remember learning how to cook
with my sister.

READER #3: My sister and I used to share secrets
and laugh together.

96

READER #4: My sister taught me how to swim.

READER #5: Every now and then, my sister and I
get together and just talk and talk.

READER #1: My sister took care of me when our
mother went to work.

READER #2: My sister and I were always together
when we were kids.

READER #3: My sister took my side when
I got into fights.

(CHORUS) I WISH I HAD A SISTER! *(Repeat)*

Slight pause.

READER #4: Why, you **can** have a sister!
A sister is just like a good friend —
and a good friend is like a sister.

READER #5: You can have all the sisters you want.
You can create your **own** sisters.

READER #4: I'd like to be your sister — take my hand.

*Each reader in turn holds out her hand to someone in the group and says: " **I'd like to be your sister — take my hand.**"*

*At this point, all five women walk over to the audience or larger group and hold out their hands, repeating: "**I'd like to be your sister; take my hand.**"*

Eventually everyone is involved in saying the words and taking hands.

Dorothy Satir wrote this for the Women and Religion Task Force, Pacific Central District, Unitarian Universalist Association.

GEORGE SAND:

DEVIANT EXTRAORDINAIRE

Dramatic Reading

by

Meg Bowman

> *"What will become of the world when all women are like George Sand?"*
> —*Balzac*

Self-portrait of George Sand
(1804-1876)

CAST:

George Sand: At age 70, she is a little hard of hearing,
(Aurore) but healthy, happy and filled with great
energy.

A little over 5' tall, she has an olive
complexion and is dressed in fashionable
female French attire of 1875.

Maurice Sand: Her son, 52, is dressed in casual attire,
such as a French aristocrat of the 1870s
would wear.

Voice On/or Off Stage:

Can be either male or female.

GEORGE SAND by Delacroix

<u>PROPS:</u>

1 Desk (or table)
2 chairs
1 cognac bottle
1 glass

A <u>desk</u> or a <u>table</u> and a <u>chair</u> where George Sand is writing.
On the desk is <u>paper</u>, perhaps a <u>container with water</u> *(for
stubbing out her cigarettes)*, a <u>bottle</u> of cognac and a <u>glass</u>.
A <u>chair</u> for her son, Maurice, to sit.

George Sand's writing desk at Nohant.

*The walls and gate to **Nohant** (on the right) with the village church in front.*

TIME: June, 1875.

PLACE: The study in <u>Nohant,</u> a large chateau located near the Indre River in the beautiful Noire Valley *(about 150 miles southwest of Paris in the Province of Berry; between Chateaurous and La Chatre).*

<u>Nohant</u> is the estate of George Sand, the most famous *(and most controversial)* author in France, if not all of Europe.

*Chateau of **Nohant**, front and entrance drive.*

105

Maurice Sand

Lina Calamatta Sand

George Sand: The most gifted woman of the 19th century.
(1804-1876)

Photographs by Nadar

The year is 1875.

GEORGE SAND, 70, is sitting at her desk, writing. On the desk are several sheets of paper, a bowl with water in it *(where she stubs out cigarettes)*, a bottle of cognac and a glass. Although a soft spoken woman, she speaks loudly enough to be heard by the audience.

Her beloved son, MAURICE SAND, 52, a successful illustrator, political cartoonist, artist, and author, is off-stage. He has just returned from a trip to Paris.

George Sand in her later years.

Aurore's grandmother, <u>Madame Dupin de Francueil</u>

(Aurore de Saxe)

<u>Hippolyte Chatiron</u>

pastel by Aurore de Saxe

<u>Aurore Dupin</u>

pastel by Aurore de Saxe

<u>VOICE ON/ or OFF STAGE:</u>

George (JOR' ZH) Sand. What an odd name for a woman.

Born **Aurore Dupin*** (O' ROR DU'PAN-- *pronounced like Chopin*) in 1804, George Sand lived a full life.

She was a workaholic, a lover of Nature, a self-proclaimed Socialist, and a somewhat liberated woman *(she couldn't understand the importance of women having the vote and a voice in government)*.

She was not beautiful, but she **was** brilliant.

Aurore (O'ROR) left an unhappy marriage and moved from her country estate to Paris where she cross-dressed, smoked cigars, changed her name, and had several affairs, including a nine-year relationship with the pale and tuber-cular Frederic Chopin (SHO' PAN) whom she called "the little one." Her affection was more maternal than sexual as she often considered Chopin her "second son."

George Sand was a Romantic who lived her life with one crisis after another. She was a trailblazer for sexual and economic freedom for women; she taught by example.

She became an author because she needed money and she wrote over 100 volumes of fiction, prose, plays, auto-biographies, letters, essays..

* *Her full name was Amatine Lucile Aurore Dupin Dudevant (or Amandine Lucie Aurore Dupin, baroness Dudevant).*

Bibliothèque Historique de la Ville de Paris, photo Lalance

<u>Solange and Maurice</u> *--by Nancy Merienne*

George Sand was the most well-known author in Europe and, yes, her work was read in the United States.

She wrote romantic novels. She was the Danielle Steele of her day.

Balzac, Matthew Arnold, Ralph Waldo Emerson, Henry James, and Victor Hugo praised her work. She influenced Jane Austen, the Brontes, Hawthorne, George Eliot *(who was a woman)* and the Russian authors Dostoyevsky (DOS' TOE-EV' SKI) and Ivan Turgeniev (TUR-GE' NEV) *(who visited George Sand at her home)*. German lyric poet Heinrich Heine became one of her closest friends; Flaubert (FLAW'-BEAR) considered her his best friend and openly wept at her funeral.*

Her works remain classics to this day, but her life exceeded the imagination of her pen.

Her son, Maurice, adored his mother and her "daughter from hell," the jealous Solange (SO'LAHN-ZH), gave her mother nothing but trouble and heartache.

This Dramatic Reading takes place in 1875 at Nohant, the country chateau where Aurore (AH'ROR) spent her child-hood.

Let's listen to a fictional conversation between George Sand at age 70 and her beloved son, Maurice, who is now 52 years old.

* *Turgeniev wrote to his friend Flaubert when he heard the news of George Sand's death: "Poor, dear Madame Sand. She loved both of us... What a heart of gold she had! What absence of every petty, mean, or false feeling! What a brave man she was, and what a good woman."*

111

Remember, it is the year 1875, a year before George Sand's death.

Let's go to the French countryside, to the comfortable manor house known as Nohant.... (NO' AHN)

The front entrance of Nohant.

MAURICE   (CALLING FROM OFF STAGE)

Ma-**ma'**, Ma-**ma'**...

Where are you?

GEORGE   (LOOKING UP FROM HER WRITING)

In here, Maurice.

(I'm) in my study.

MAURICE   (ENTERS)

I might have known.

Ah, Mother, I've just returned from Paris.
(The) roads are insufferable....
 I've never seen so many pot holes.

(But,) I just had to be here to celebrate
 our birthdays....*
Can you believe it ?
My 52nd and your 70th!

(EMBRACES AND KISSES HIS
MOTHER ON BOTH CHEEKS)

What are you writing?

** Maurice Sand was born June 30, 1823 and his
mother,Aurore Dupin (George Sand) was born July 1,
1804. They often celebrated their birthdays on July 6th.*

GEORGE   Letters, of course.

            (I have) finished a new edition of my novel
            "Valentine".... which I have dedicated to
            Victor Hugo. We're great pen pals.

MAURICE   No new children's novels?

GEORGE   Maurice! In the last three years, I have
            written 13 novels for children.
            Enough! Enough!

MAURICE   (LAUGHING)

            Well, your granddaughters adore them.

GEORGE   And I adore **them!**
            I'm so glad that you, Lina* — and the girls
            live here at Nohant (NO' AHN).

* *Marcelina Calamatta married Maurice Sand in 1862*
when she was 20 and he was 39 years old. She was the
daughter of a Paris engineer (of Italian descent) and had a
lively wit.

Sit down, my dear.*
Would you like a cognac?

(MOTIONS TOWARD BOTTLE
ON HER DESK)

MAURICE   (SITS DOWN ON A CHAIR)

No, thanks, Ma-**ma'**.**

GEORGE   I love an old cognac.... **and** a good cigar.

Where **are** those two darling daughters
of yours?

MAURICE   In the kitchen.... *(I)* can't believe Lolo
is nine years old, and little Gabriella?
(She's) destined to be a great beauty. ***

*   *Feel free to use French phrases, such as "mon cher" instead of "my dear", "oui" (WE) instead of "yes", and "merci" (MER-SEE') instead of "thank you."*

**   <u>Option:</u> *Maurice accepts a glass of cognac.*

*** *Aurore (also known as Lolo') married in 1889 (1866-1961); Gabriella (1868-1909) did, indeed, develop into a beautiful woman and married in 1890. Neither daughter had children.*

GEORGE   I have sewn several new dresses for them.
           You know, Maurice, I **love** being their tutor.

MAURICE   You love **spoiling** them.... clothes, toys,
           ponies....

           Aren't you glad I waited until I was 39
           before I married?

GEORGE   I'm glad you waited for Lina. Your wife is
           "the pearl" in this house. A real treasure,
           my "true" daughter.

MAURICE   And Solange?   Your daughter from hell?

GEORGE   *(She was)* here again this morning, ordering
           servants about, telling outrageous stories....
           and now she lives only two miles away!

           Oh, what did I do to deserve such a
           daughter?

MAURICE   Well, at least Solange chooses rich men
           to sleep with.

GEORGE   Do we call her courtesane (KOR' TAH
           ZAN) or whore?

MAURICE   We call her the **most famous courtesane**
            in all France!

            And we call her beautiful, clever, witty....
            and selfish, malicious, greedy, and spoiled.

GEORGE   A snob, and "the Queen of Sloths."

MAURICE   *(Is she)* still begging money?

GEORGE   Constantly.... Despite her allowance from
            me, her inheritance from her father, her
            millionaire lovers.... it's **never** enough.

MAURICE   Oh, Ma-**ma'**, such a generous heart.
            But then, you **always** give **everyone**
            too much money.
            You know, Solange received **a lot**
            of money when Pa-**pa'** died....

GEORGE   Maybe her wild antics are genetic.
            My mother was unstable, given to tantrums,
            and **always** needed money.

MAURICE   Was Sophie **really** a gypsy?

117

GEORGE   Could be. God, how I loved that woman!*

           (She was) a penniless camp follower with
           a child when Pa-**pa**' fell in love with her.

           Her father sold birds on the streets of Paris.

MAURICE   And **your** father was of the aristocracy.**

*   *Sophie Victoire Antoinette Delaborde (1773 -1837), mistress to a general in the French army, had a daughter named Caroline Delaborde (Cazamajou) born 1799 and thus six years older than her half-sister, Aurore (George Sand). Sophie secretly married Maurice Dupin and when pregnant with Aurore (George Sand) was introduced to his mother, Aurore de Saxe (1748-1821) who disapproved of her only son marrying the emotional, flightly, unstable daughter of a street peddler of birds.*

** *Maurice Dupin (1778-1804), George Sand's father, was an only son to Aurore de Saxe and her second husband (she was 30 and he was 62 years old when they married; the devoted couple had ten years of happiness together before he died). His paternal great grandfather, Maurice de Saxe, illigitimate son of the king of Poland, became recognized as the greatest General (Marshal of France) of his age. He also became quite wealthy.*

GEORGE   An officer of the French army.

              (He) played violin.... Magnificent voice.
              Spoiled me.... and *(he was)* **very
              possessive** of my mother.

              Of course, Grandma-**ma'** did **not** want
              her only son to marry this emotional
              "bird seller" woman.

MAURICE   I remember your mother as shrewd and
              quick tempered, charming one minute and
              then....

GEORGE   Passionate and quite mad, but I loved her.

MAURICE   Then, when you were only four....

GEORGE   Pa-**pa'** was thrown from a horse
              and died *(from)* a broken neck.

              For the next 14 years, I was the center
              of a tug of war between Ma-**ma'** and
              Grandma-**ma'**.

              Little Aurore (AH' ROR) Dudevant, the
              princess of this lovely valley.

MauriceDupin
George Sand's father.

Sophia Dupin
(pencil sketch by George Sand)
George Sand's mother.

Aurore and Casimir Dudevant *(by Francois Biard)*

120

MAURICE   Noire (NU'-WHAR) Valley **is** beautiful.
           I love this view, the walnut trees, the river,
           the clean air....

GEORGE   *(It)* broke my heart when Mother left me
           here and went to Paris. Of course,
           Grandma-**ma'** had paid her handsomely.

MAURICE   Your grandmother taught you to love music
           and nature.

GEORGE   And she taught me logic. Grandma-**ma'**
           was a freethinker. *(She)* read John Locke
           and Voltaire, *(and)* corresponded with
           Rousseau; he visited here.... many times.

           (PAUSE)

           By age four, I could read. By age five,
           I had taught myself how to write.

           (I) had a pet donkey.... and a tutor....
           Learned **six** languages!

           How I loved the harp.... and novels,
           Greek myths, fairy tales.
           (I) used to make up stories, and
           I guess I've play-acted all my life.

MAURICE   Ma-**ma**', when did you start writing novels?

GEORGE   *(In)* my teens. Always had stories
in my head. Ah, *(I was)* so active then.
Used to ride all over this valley, and **not**
side-saddle! Wore boys' clothes.
Talked to everyone. Such freedom!

MAURICE   Why did your grandmother send you
to a Catholic convent?

GEORGE   Politics, my dear.
It was a **British** convent in Paris.
That's where I learned English ....
and picked up our custom
of afternoon tea.

You see, Maurice, Napoleon was defeated,
the Church and the aristocracy were back
in power, **so** for appearances' sake, I was
cloistered in that **cold** prison.
Winter mornings, I had to break the ice
in my basin.

Our windows were covered so we couldn't
look outside. I felt abandoned.

Sister Alippe (AH LEEP') called me
a Pagan.

Religion seemed so ridiculous....
I resolved to never take it seriously.

But I did have an amazing "mystical
experience" — an hallucination — and
Grandma-**ma**', fearing I was becoming
"pickled in God," brought me back here
to Nohant.

(And) just when I had started having fun
writing and directing plays!

But Grandma-**ma**' was ailing and wanted
me **properly** married before she died.
I was about 16.

MAURICE   Is that when you married Pa-**pa**'?

GEORGE   With my large dowry, the matchmakers
went to work.
A 40 year old baron?
A 50 year old fool with a saber cut across
his face?

But Grandma-**ma**' suffered a stroke
and was bedridden.
How I **loved** taking care of that dear lady.

I **had to** manage the chateau and the mills,
the land, the tenants....

MAURICE   You always were self-reliant, independent....

GEORGE   Her last words to me were,
          (SLOWLY)
          "You are losing your best friend."

          (PAUSE)

MAURICE   When **did** you meet Pa-**pa**'?

GEORGE   Well, after the funeral, Mother arrived.
          (I) hadn't seen her in four years.
          (She was) so erratic.... so jealous of my
          education. *(She)* snatched books out of
          my hand.

          (She) made me her servant....
           I waited on her hand and foot,
           but she did teach me how to sew.
          Well, I became ill, a fever.
           She pocketed my year's allowance
           and dumped me with friends.... for months!

          I was so unhappy.

          Oh, I had many offers of marriage.
          Everyone considered **me** a good deal....
          this beautiful estate, lots of money.

I was 18 when I met Casimir *(Dudevant)*. *

As you know, your father **wasn't** handsome,
but we became friends.
When we married, French law gave **him**
control of **all** my inherited land, buildings,
income....

He took women for granted.

Big mistake!

MAURICE   Ah, but Ma-**ma**', you had me and Solange.

GEORGE   Yes, my dear. *(And)* how I doted on you.

I insisted on nursing you.
I loved being a mother!
For over 300 years, aristocrats
had hired wet nurses. **Not me!**

MAURICE   I remember playing at your feet
as you read.

* *Baron Francois (Casimir) Dudevant (DU-DEH-VAN'*
or DUD'VAHN), a local nobleman, (1795-1871)
was 27 when he married Aurore, 18.

GEORGE   I was a meek, dutiful, and bored
          housewife. Sometimes, I would
          just saddle up a horse and ride all day!

          I was miserable with Casimir.
          Sex was a duty; I was never aroused.

MAURICE   Pa-**pa**' and Uncle Hippolyte (IP OH
           LEET) * were terrible drunks
          (They were) so loud.
          All they did was hunt and drink.

GEORGE   Your father **couldn't** manage the estate.
          Oh, the debts!

          And, he cut down the woods!

          Then, one day, I happened upon your
          father's will. I was stunned — he hated **me**!

*   *Hippolyte Chatiron (1798-1848), six years older than
     Aurore, was her father's illegitimate son by a servant
     girl. Even as a child, Hippolyte was resentful, brutal
     and cruel. As an adult, he became a crying drunk who
     went on weeping jags. His wife spent most of her time
     sleeping in their house (Chateau de Montgivray) located
     about two miles from Nohant. Solange, George Sand's
     daughter, bought and moved into this house in 1873.*

But, the final straw was while I was resting after the birth of Solange. My drunken half-brother, yes, Hippolyte (IP OH LEET'), passed out on the floor. My drunken husband noisily having sex with a servant girl he had trapped in the adjoining sitting room.

I **knew** I had to leave.

Well, I asked for only a small allowance.... a pitiful few coins.... to live in Paris for half a year. Hippolyte laughed, said I would starve... *(and)* come crawling back.

MAURICE   I remember when you and Baby Solange left and I stayed here with Pa-**pa'**. Uncle Hippolyte told me you would never come back.

GEORGE   So cruel.

I know, I know....
Your father never took an interest in you, but I **had** to flee.
Oh, the tears of despair!

I **needed** to discuss literature, philosophy, ideas....
I had met Jules Sandeau (SAHN DOE'), and he had fallen in love with me.

127

Early days in Paris. <u>Aurore Dudevant</u> with a friend.

I was starved for affection....
and I discovered that women could
actually enjoy sex.
We took a three room garret apartment
(on the) top floor— with a balcony—
(we) could see the Notre Dame.
But, oh, five flights of stairs, **no** maid —
I did all the washing....

MAURICE *(That was)* Paris, back in the 1830s.

GEORGE *(There was)* great political ferment.
Artists and intellectuals *(were)* crying out
for a democratic republic.

Me wanting to go to meetings and
restaurants, but women weren't allowed.

I hungered to go to the theatre, but women
had to pay far more than men **and then**
sit with escorts in a certain section.

MAURICE And that's why you dressed
in men's clothing.

GEORGE Yes, for freedom!

Besides, my thin shoes wore out
after two days on the paving stones.

And spattered mud ruined my velvet
dresses.

So, I just wore sturdy boots and trousers
and a vest.... sometimes a long coat....
(I) concealed my long hair beneath a broad-
brimmed hat....

Lowered my voice and **voila'**! (VWA-LA')
Freedom to come and go as I pleased!
How I **loved** those steel-tipped boots.
At last, I was solid on the sidewalk!

MAURICE   I missed you so much.

GEORGE   And I missed you, my son, but I **needed**
to earn money.
Painting cigar boxes wasn't enough,
so I wrote.
If I could write **letters**, I felt I could
write **novels**.

MAURICE   When you returned home,
you almost smothered me with kisses.
I was wearing the uniform you sent me.

GEORGE   My big seven year old, so handsome
            with the red plumed headdress.

MAURICE   You taught me Latin, and we tamed birds.

GEORGE   And I wrote, re-wrote, edited. I was a
            keen observer and I was determined —
            I had a passion — to have a literary career.

MAURICE   And you took me back to Paris with you.

GEORGE   My first novel "Indiana" by **Mister**
            George Sand was a smashing success!
            Balzac gave it the highest praises.

MAURICE   I remember when people discovered
            George Sand was a woman.

GEORGE   Yes, I used the name **George** because it
            means "a man of the Earth" and the name
            Sand from my lover, Sandeau.

MAURICE   He was so jealous of you.
            And what a brat Solange was.

Do you remember that cold winter day
in Paris — in the carriage — when she
threw her shoes out... into the bushes?

And what a flirt! Every man in sight!
Ma-**ma**', I fear you were too busy to notice.

GEORGE   Writing articles, essays, short stories,
            25 plays, almost 60 novels....

MAURICE   Over 100 all together.

            Ma-**ma**', you're the most well-read author
            in Europe.

GEORGE   Not one book a failure.
            I knew what the public wanted — romance.

MAURICE   Famous overnight.... A celebrity!

GEORGE   "Leila" was translated into six languages,
            including English. *(It was)* almost
            autobiographical.

            Ah, lots of sex in that book. **Shocking!**

MAURICE   Many a husband— even Pa-**pa**' — sobered
           up long enough to read **that** book.

           And then threaten you.

GEORGE   Yes, I became the subject of much idle
           gossip. But women **should** enjoy sex.
           Men **should** marry for companionship,
           not dominance.

MAURICE   I agree, Ma-**ma**', marriage **should** be
           a partnership.

GEORGE   As a child, I read Aristotle and Plato....
           both took the superiority of men for granted.
           St. Paul and St. Augustine **disliked** women.
           I remember a priest coming here using
           scripture to prove men were superior.

           Such nonsense!

           And then I read the plays of Racine and
           Moliere'. Men were aggressors and women
           objects of men's passions. My mother
           bought into that idea— women *(are)* subject
           to the lusts of men.

George Sand with a fan
(colored drawing by Alfred de Musset)

Alfred de Musset smoking a cigar
(by himself)

134

And my darling Grandma-**ma**', who always
spoke with such candor — widowed at
15, married off to two men, both twice
her age — said, 'Women have **no choice**.'

Well, I was **determined** to have choices
in my life!

Then, I fell in love with Alfred
(de Musset) and we went to Italy.
Ah, Venice, city of my dreams....

MAURICE   And, as usual, you paid for everything.

GEORGE   He had no money!

(I) kept on writing — two novels and a
novelette. Alfred called me a bore and
left to explore the dives and brothels
of Venice.
He could be so sweet, so tender —
then violent, petty, selfish.

So handsome.... Ah, I was madly in love....

MAURICE   Ah, Ma-**ma**, you know, you usually
chose young, slender, handsome men...
weak men... in need of nurturing...
and money.

135

GEORGE   I know, I know....
            (I was) the dominant one.

            Alfred wandered the slums of Venice,
            drunk, fighting.... then became ill.

MAURICE   And, of course, you nursed him.

GEORGE   Called a doctor.... and.... (LAUGHS)
            the doctor fell in love **with me!**
            Such Romantics!

MAURICE   I remember when you returned to Paris.
            Solange and I were in school then.

GEORGE   I was caught up in Alfred's jealous
            rages. Such passion, such remorse.
            I was obsessed!
            Then he yelled, " I **never** loved you!"
            (I was) so hurt and humiliated....

            Franz Liszt tried to console me.

            I took scissors to my long hair and sent
            the shorn locks to Alfred.

MAURICE   Ma-**ma'**, you **didn't!**

136

GEORGE   Heartbroken, I retreated back here.
          But your father was so **despotic**,
          so **dissipated**.... **lewd**.... **and** losing money.
          I felt that **neither** my house **nor** my
          children belonged to me.

          (I) consulted a lawyer and **finally**
          Casimir signed a paper.
          I gave him my house in Paris, half my
          inheritance, but **I kept this house**
          (Nohant).
          Then, he changed his mind; wanted more
          money. What a mess!

MAURICE   You always hated family bickering.
           I have never heard you raise your voice.

          You always seem to be in control, so calm.

          Remember the time Pa-**pa'** insulted you?
          We had dinner guests. Then, you tried
          to protect me, and Pa-**pa'** went to strike
          you and hit a guest?

          He thundered, (LOUDLY)
          "I am the master of this house!"

GEORGE   And then ran for a gun.

            Even if it meant public scandal,
            I **needed** a legal separation.

            Oh! The multitudes of women trapped
             in loveless marriages!

            We need a revolution!

MAURICE   Pa-**pa'** demanded a trial, and drew up
            a petition listing 10 years of your
            transgressions.

            What a **sensation** that was!

GEORGE   The estate was almost bankrupt,
            but Nohant was declared mine,
            and I won custody of Solange.
            But, oh, the debts!

MAURICE   You *(have)* always supported
             so many people.

            Our servants have always had the
            highest pay plus generous pensions.

            No wonder you were always writing,
            writing, writing....

GEORGE   I never needed much sleep.... a night person.
(I) still write from around 11 or midnight
until daylight --at least 10 to 20 pages.

(Then) sleep until 9, breakfast at 10....
take care of correspondence, take my
walk.... time for guests and then....

MAURICE   ....dinner at 8.

Ma-**ma**', do you remember the summer
of 1836?
I was 13 and we went to Switzerland
to visit Franz Liszt?

GEORGE   Oh, the concerts that man gave to raise
money for *(the)* striking workers of Lyon
(LEE- OHN)!
We **longed** to see a democratic government
in France.

MAURICE   We climbed the glaciers on donkeys.
Sometimes, you and Solange wore
men's clothes....
We played jokes on one another.

GEORGE   And had picnics every day.

MAURICE   You really shocked people
           by smoking cigars in public.

GEORGE   And I would stretch out on the floor
           beneath the piano when Liszt played
           his new compositions...
           Truly "enveloped" (EN-VEL'-UPED)
           by music.

MAURICE   *(It was)* a delightful summer....
           Then, back to Paris and school.

GEORGE   Back to Paris and the salons,
           conversations, music...
           Poets—Heinreich Heine... Painters—
           Delacroix (DEH LAH CRAH')...
           Writers—Balzac...

MAURICE   I think that most of those men were
           in love with you.

GEORGE   Ah, Maurice, when my letters began to
           appear in print, those **freethinking** men
           had second thoughts; it hadn't occurred
           to them that their ideals of human equality
           include **women**.

MAURICE   Your contention that corruption does
           not come from being human,
           but from **social** conditions
           was shocking, too.

GEORGE   But **not** as shocking as my love for
           Marie Dorval (DOR-VAHL').

MAURICE   Ah, yes, she was really beautiful...
           (with) long blue-black hair.
           (The) most famous actress in France.

GEORGE   Such talent!
           She was wonderful as Lady Macbeth.
           It was 1833 when I wrote that fan letter....
           Our friendship lasted 16 years—
           until her death.

           Oh, the gossip, the rumors.
           We met secretly.

MAURICE   Her Sunday dinners were the greatest!

GEORGE   So charming. The fairest of them all.
           With her I felt so alive.
           We were inseparable friends....
           and lovers.

Marie Dorval
(lithograph by Jean Gigoux)

Marie Dorval
(by Leon Noel)

Yes, my most satisfying sexual
relationship was with Marie Dorval.

MAURICE   She died really young.

GEORGE   Only 51.... in 1848.
            I promised to take care of her three
            daughters, and the grandchildren.

MAURICE   *(You)* gave them the best education
            possible.

            How they loved coming here for
            summer holidays!

GEORGE   I think *(that)* the greatest crime against
            women is **not** giving them a good
            education.

            You know, Maurice, I never deceived
            anyone. I have known utter and
            complete love — not once, many times —
            but *(had)* only one lover at a time.

            However, I think if I could begin my life
            again, I would elect to remain chaste.

143

MAURICE   Ma-**ma**'! It's **too late now**!!!!

GEORGE   Well, I did crusade for sexual freedom.

MAURICE   And outraged the middle class.

GEORGE   But I was always feminine,
took care of the family....

MAURICE   ....an excellent cook.

Ma-**ma**', you always made our
home a comfortable refuge.

Liszt and his Marie* spent the summer
here — 1837 — the year....

GEORGE   .... the year my mother died.
I rushed back to Paris.

Sophie didn't want sour looking priests
at the end, she wanted smiling faces.

(PAUSE)

* *Marie d'Agoult. Later, she also used a male nom de plum to publish books.*

144

MAURICE   That was the winter Balzac came here.
            (He was) so witty.... so earthy.
            I loved his fat belly!

GEORGE   Always bursting with tales
            and laughter....

MAURICE   He often said he could discuss any subject
            with you.

GEORGE   I gave him the idea for his novel "Beatrix,"
            the romance of Liszt and Marie.
            He put me in that novel, too. *

MAURICE   Then, you captured the heart of Frederic
            Chopin (SHO' PAN).

GEORGE   Strange how Chopin and I disagreed on
            almost every subject, but we both loved
            music....

            He trusted me completely until Solange
            told those awful lies.

*   *As Camille Maupin.*

145

The Monastery at Valldemosa.

photo from the F Chopin and G. Sand collection; presented by Mme. A. M. Ferrá

In an orange grove in Majorca, <u>Maurice and Solange</u> "stuff themselves with oranges." Drawing by Maurice Sand.

146

MAURICE   And he expected you to take care of him.

GEORGE   Oh, but Maurice, he was in such
           delicate health.

MAURICE   I know, I know....

           You dragged us off to the island of
           Majorca* (MY YORK' AH).

           I think I was 16 then.
           A warmer climate, you said.

           Ha! We almost froze **and**
           we almost drowned!

GEORGE   But you, my darling, grew robust
           and healthy.

           And, Solange stopped being so
           troublesome.

MAURICE   It rained for weeks!
           We were evicted when word spread
           that Chopin had consumption.

* *Mallorca*

147

Remember the deserted monastery atop the mountain? With all the secret passages and the caves?

GEORGE   It was the **only** place we could go!

MAURICE   We were pariahs (PAH RYE' AHZ).
           Heathens who didn't attend Mass.

           Isolated by hostile locals; no servants.
           You had to do **all** the work.

           But Solange and I had a grand time.
           Exploring, eating oranges....
           and we adored Chopin.

GEORGE   He wrote his most famous sonatas,
           nocturnes, mazurkas in our monastery.

MAURICE   And when we came home, he got us
           started performing amateur theatre
           here.... almost every night.
           The plays you wrote were such fun.

GEORGE   Maurice, **you** built the stage, the lights,
           carved the puppets.... *(and)* **you** wrote
           many of the sketches.

148

MAURICE	Our theatre holds 50 guests. How I love it when you — and our guests — perform.
GEORGE	And **I** love sewing the costumes.
MAURICE	And I love our summers here at Nohant. Remember when Chopin closed himself up in the music room to re-write a measure, sometimes a hundred times.
GEORGE	I think he wrote his most **beautiful** Sonatas here...Sonata in B-Flat Minor....
	Ah, we were together for over eight years. So devoted.... A loving friendship. From passion to compassion to pity, but *(we)* always encouraged each other.
	He had velvet fingers. Ah, those evenings.... those marvelous countryside walks.
MAURICE	When I decided to become an artist, Chopin always complimented my efforts.
GEORGE	He played cards with Solange....

149

Chopin
(sketch by George Sand)

Frederic Chopin in 1838.
(Portrait by Delacroix)

GEORGE SAND in 1838
(by Delacrois)

MAURICE   I remember those evenings. You
correcting proofs or stitching a costume,
friends mounting specimens, sketching,
writing comic verse.... playing chess,
charades, dominoes, word games.......
reading aloud, the music.

GEORGE   *(But)* by midnight, I had retired
to my study and wrote 'til dawn....

Usually, I was terribly in debt.
Remember the time my publisher dropped
me.... when I submitted two, well,
rather **radical** novels.

Everyone knows I'm a socialist,
but they called me a **communist!**

MAURICE   Well, that was a new word coming
into vogue.

GEORGE   *(I)* started a periodical.... and serialized
a new novel, but after 150 chapters
I was exhausted....   Migraines.

Chopin was so ill, depressed, so jealous.
Solange was so extravagant.

151

By then, I had adopted your cousin, Augustine....

Dozens of people depended on me.

MAURICE   I really liked Chopin.

GEORGE   I think you were about 24 when Chopin left. Solange must have been around 19. What a head-strong golden-haired beauty!

MAURICE   What an outrageous, spiteful liar she was.... And most of the lies she told Chopin were about **you**! *(She)* said **you** instigated the scene when Solange and her despicable husband stole the furniture, bedspreads, candelabra... from upstairs... and Chopin believed her!

GEORGE   What an uproar!
Yes, poor Chopin died* not knowing they were lies.

MAURICE   Solange had married that drunken sculptor, Clesinger. What a disaster!

* *Chopin died in 1849, a little over a year after he left George Sand.*

152

GEORGE   But I loved their little girl, Nini
          (NEE-NEE).*

MAURICE   Solange **used** little Nini to get money
          from you. The 3,000 gold francs you gave
          her each year were squandered on lavish
          parties, new furniture, liquor....

GEORGE   It was **never** enough.

          Then, after Solange's husband divorced her,
           I got custody of little Nini.
          We were inseparable.

          How I doted on that darling little girl.
          Her death was totally unnecessary.

MAURICE   Only nine years old.
          We were all grief striken.

GEORGE   Clesinger, that idiot, took Nini out of
          school on that bitterly cold, windy day
          without a wrap. She died from
          scarlet fever... pneumonia....

* *Jeanne-Gabrielle Clesinger (1849-1855).*

MAURICE   I worried about your mental and physical
            health.... We **needed** that trip to Italy.

GEORGE   I always loved Italy *(but)* hated Rome—
            a disgusting medley of ugliness and filth—
            beggars everywhere;
            everyone out to cheat tourists.

            The oppression by the clergy depressed
            me even more!

MAURICE   Then you wrote your memoirs....*

GEORGE   Yes, I was in debt again.

            And remember the revolution?
            The overthrow of the French monarchy?

* She wrote <u>Story of My Life</u> in 1854-1855 (138 installments
in <u>La Presse</u> (Paris) which was published in 20 volumes.
These memoirs were translated into English and put into one
readable volume <u>George Sand: My Life</u> by Dan Hofstadter
(Harper & Row, 1979).

154

MAURICE   Yes, summer, 1848.

           Potato blight, peasants suffering, workers'
           salaries cut more than half, unemploy-
           ment...

GEORGE   **Even** the smug bourgeoisie
           (BUR ZWAH' ZEE') who owned the
           factories were sick of the royalty.

MAURICE   Oh, the demonstrations, barricades,
           50 demonstrators shot....
            But the National Guard refused
            to fire on the people.

           Vive la republique!

GEORGE   **VIVE LA REPUBLIQUE!**

           And I became the Minister of Propaganda
           for the new republic.

           Worked 16 hours a day!
           Wrote proclamations, circulars....
           I felt **so alive**, so strong....

MAURICE   And I became mayor of the village
           here at Nohant.

GEORGE   Then, warring political factions.
Factions within factions!
God! I hate war! I hate bloodshed....
(and) killing!

(Alexis) de Tocqueville (DEH TOKE' VIL)
considered me an enemy when I urged him
to **not** push the people to a breaking point.

MAURICE   They used bayonets to arrest workers.

GEORGE   And I was advised to flee the country.
Instead, I came here.

MAURICE   Over 25,000 workers arrested, thousands
killed....

Repression.

Then, in 1851, a coup d'etat (COO DEY'
TAH)... *(the)* legislature dissolved,
 a reign of terror, deportations, executions....

The republic was lost.

GEORGE   And **I** was blamed for the class war in Paris!
All our friends were in danger.

MAURICE   Bless you, Ma'ma.
            You dared to go to Paris and plead
            for your friends....
            get them released from prison.
            How I feared for your safety.

GEORGE   Robert and Elizabeth Barrett Browning
            came to visit and were surprised to see
            me so preoccupied, **so serious.**

            (But) I stopped deportations and managed
            to get sick prisoners released.

MAURICE   Everyone was relieved when
            you came home.

GEORGE   More incensed than ever over injustices.

            (I) wrote the preface to the French
            edition of Harriet Beecher Stowe's book,
            "Uncle Tom's Cabin."

MAURICE   Then came the government censorship
            in the 1850s.

GEORGE   And **I** was in **my 50s**, an "old woman"....
             My romantic youth behind me, well....
             almost.*

             I'll never forget what Charles Dickens
             wrote after I met him at a dinner party.
             (He) said I was nothing more than "an
             ordinary woman in appearance and
             manners."

             It was **then** I decided to live my life
             for **others**.... *(for)* those who need me.

MAURICE   And became known as "The Good Lady
             of Nohant."

GEORGE   *(I)* published "<u>The Story of My Life</u>"
              and ten plays.

MAURICE   And the great Sarah Bernhardt played
             the leading role in **three** of them.

* *The last of her lovers included Manceau whom she nursed
for five months before his death from tuberculosis in 1865,
Charles Marchal, and a young feminist writer (1868), Juliette
Adam.*

GEORGE   I wonder if people know how **anti**-clerical
          I really am?

          When my play "Le Marquis (LEH
          MAR'KEY) opened in Paris about six
          years ago... yes, 1864.... those organized
          religious groups planned demonstrations
          against it.

MAURICE   And students came out by the thousands
          chanting **"Long Live George Sand!"**

GEORGE   Such thunderous applause.
          Hundreds came to shake my hand...
          and kiss me.

          Imagine! In my 60s and all that praise.

          Welcomed everywhere! Even in
          restaurants... **even** in a dress!
          Perhaps I was wrong when I opposed
          women in the Senate and Armed Forces,
          saying they had no business in the Literary
          Academy.... those **all-male** sanctuaries.

          Women vote? I felt they had the cart before
          the horse. I felt that **first** women needed
          equality within marriage, **then** political
          rights.

159

Actually, Maurice, I feared being
the laughing stock of the country!

MAURICE   Many women were disappointed when you
            refused to be a candidate for the
            Assembly.

            You were a household name....
            calling attention to women's **in**equality.

GEORGE   I **know** I am the equal of man.

            I **never** flattered men, played coy,
            used feminine trickery.

            If only women dealt openly with men.
            We need candor!

            But I will never live to see it!

MAURICE   Nor I.

GEORGE   Well, I need to finish this letter to
            Gustave....

MAURICE   How is your friend Flaubert (FLAW-
            BEAR)?

160

GEORGE   *(He's)* pudgy, balding, myopic... but I
                 love his masterpiece "Madam Bovary."

MAURICE   Well, I **love** the fairy tales you've
                 been writing!

GEORGE   You know, Maurice, when I die
                 Solange will shove your wife aside
                 and take over the estate

                 Mark my words.

MAURICE   I'm glad Lina was here to care for you
                 when you had the flu last year.

GEORGE   Lina is a treasure, but except for a touch
                 of rheumatism and stomach problems
                 now and then... I'm hale and hearty.

                 My hands are steady.... *(and I)*
                 still take a daily swim in the river.
                 (I) keep writing... two or three books a year.

                 Maurice, if I do take sick and those doctors
                 declare me dead, be sure to check
                 carefully....
                 I fear being buried alive.

Frederic Chopin (age 36)　　　*George Sand (age 33) by Julien c. 1837*

Maurice Sand (age14) 1837　　　*Solange Sand (age 19) 1847*

(by Luigi Calamatta)　　　*(by J..B. Clesinger)*

MAURICE   Ah, that's a long-time fear of yours...

                Well, **I** fear Solange descending and taking over everything.

GEORGE   She **would** give me a church service, wouldn't she?

GEORGE SAND GOES INTO A FREEZE POSITION.

MAURICE STANDS AND READS THE FOLLOWING:

A year later, in 1876, Amantine Lucile Aurore Dudevant, known as George Sand, suffered great stomach pains. Doctors bungled the treatment of a bowel obstruction and on June 8th, my mother bade us a fond farewell and died at the age of 71.

As predicted, my headstrong sister, Solange, took over, sat at the head of the table, issued an unending series of orders to the servants, and demanded a church funeral.

It rained that day.

George Sand was an honorable woman.

She spoke frankly and truthfully.

Everyone always knew where she stood.

GEORGE SAND
by *Julien Boilly*

Dumas (DOO-MAH) and Flaubert (FLAW-BEAR) openly wept at my mother's funeral and Victor Hugo said, "We know a true goddess from her stride."

I never got over my mother's death. I spent four years gathering and publishing her thousands of letters.

I died in 1889 at age 66, surviving my mother by only 13 years. Neither of the granddaughters had children. The Sand line came to an end.

Twenty-two years later, in 1898, Solange died. She, too, was 71 years old.

Today, the Nohant estate is a monument and a shrine where George Sand's forceful personality transcends the barriers of time and death.

George Sand, you had a long and rich life.
Dear Ma-**ma**', please stand and take a bow.

Brava! Brava!

GEORGE SAND STANDS AND SHE AND MAURICE BOTH TAKE A BOW SIGNALLING THE END OF THE DRAMATIC READING.

END

George Sand finally summoned the courage
to tell Victor Hugo,
"When I am in your presence,
I am stricken dumb."

Hugo replied,
"I have spent my entire life
searching for a
silent woman,
and I regret that George Sand,
the only woman of
our time whose thoughts are worth hearing,
should be that one."

"Abstinence? From what?
Enjoy the sun, the lilacs in flower.
No! Enjoy!"
　　　　　—*George Sand*

Never forget, on one side of my family is a King of Poland,
the other, my grandfather, the bird seller, and my mother,
who sold herself to men as a mistress, and who was a seam-
stress, and a Bohemian of gypsy origin.

Men Speak:

Two days after she died *(June 8, 1876)*, The Tower of Percemont was published. Flaubert, who had read the other two works printed that year, wrote to Sand: "La Tour de Percemont pleased me extremely, but Marianne has literally enchanted me."

"There is no better writer in France today."
—*Victor Hugo*

"You will be the Lord Byron of France."
—*Chateaubriant (after reading Leila)*

"The most remarkable writer of the present century..."
—*George Henry Lewes, 1842*

Auguste de Keratry, a fairly popular writer and an old man with a young wife, expounded on the inferiority of women and then told Sand, "Don't make books, make babies."

George Sand replied as she left his study, "Upon my word, sir, you should follow your own advice, if you can."

Films:

<u>Song to Remember</u> (1945) with Merle Oberon and Cornell Wilde.

<u>Impromptu</u> (1991) with Judy Davis and Hugh Grant.

"...the most womanly woman I have ever known."
              --Alfred De Musset

"...the finest female genius of any country or age."
              --Elizabeth Barrett Browning

GEORGE SAND —
(Baroness Amandine Aurore Lucie Dupin Dudevant)

"...I admired her outlandish behavior, that cigar-smoking woman who bushwhacked her way through the nineteenth century, wearing men's clothes when she went out hunting or when she attended the Paris theater. I enjoyed the stories of her amorous adventures, how she became the lover of famous composers, revolutionaries, writers, and actors, not all of them male."

WOMAN AS HEROINE

"Sand was never afraid to take unpopular positions in her novels, positions that seem advanced even today. She stands alone among nineteenth century novelists as the only writer who has given us an image of a "fallen woman"...who is *not* punished by fate, but who bounces back from being abused and seduced to become successful and loved...."

— from **Translator's Introduction**, p. vi
GEORGE SAND: HORACE
Translated by Zack Rogow (Mercury House, San Francisco, 1995).

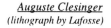

Auguste Clesinger
(lithograph by Lafosse)

Solange
(drawing by Clesinger)

Solange expressed extreme hostility toward her mother; she wanted to be more famous than George Sand.

Honore' de Balzac, 1842.

Honore' de Balzac noted that George Sand had <u>love</u>, not sex affairs; Solange had <u>sex</u>, not love affairs.

170

BIBLIOGRAPHY

Atwood, William G., THE LIONESS AND THE LITTLE ONE:
THE LIAISON OF GEORGE SAND AND FREDERIC CHOPIN
(Columbia University Press, 1980).

Barry, Joseph, ed., GEORGE SAND: IN HER OWN WORDS
(Quartet Books, 1979).

Cate, Curtis, GEORGE SAND: A BIOGRAPHY
(Houghton Mifflin Co., Boston, 1975).

Edwards, Samuel, GEORGE SAND: A BIOGRAPHY OF THE FIRST
MODERN LIBERATED WOMAN   (David McKay Co., 1972).

Hofstader, Dan *(translated and adapted by),* MY LIFE: GEORGE
SAND (Harper & Row, 1979).

Hovey, Tamara, A MIND OF HER OWN: A LIFE OF THE WRITER
GEORGE SAND (Harper & Row, 1977).

Jordan, Ruth, GEORGE SAND: A BIOGRAPHICAL PORTRAIT
(Taplinger, NY, 1976) .

Moers, Ellen, LITERARY WOMEN: THE GREAT WRITERS
(Doubleday, 1976) .

Thomson, Patricia, GEORGE SAND AND THE VICTORIANS
(Columbia University Press, 1977).

Sand, George, HORACE, translated by Zack Rogow
(Mercury House, San Francisco, 1995).

Winegarten, Renee, THE DOUBLE LIFE OF GEORGE SAND:
THE WOMAN AND WRITER (Basic Books, NY, 1978).

Winwar, Frances, THE LIFE OF THE HEART: GEORGE SAND
AND HER TIMES (Harper, 1945).

Modern Women: Please Note:

It has been said that George Sand "lived a century and a half before her time" * but **no one** is born before their time. We need a George Sand *(an Emma Goldman, Alice Paul, Elizabeth Cady Stanton, Susan B. Anthony, Margaret Sanger...)* to initiate social change, to be on the 'cutting edge.' By living her life of sexual and economic freedom, George Sand taught by example.

If **you** reject the double standard, combine a career with motherhood, demand personal autonomy, wear slacks, jeans, or pants and comfortable shoes *(or boots)*, smoke in public, enjoy sexual and economic freedom, talk to men as equals.... then **you** owe a debt to George Sand. You might also ponder Balzac's question:

"What will become of the world
when all women are like George Sand?"

---

* *George Sand: A Biography of the First Modern Liberated Woman,*
Samuel Edwards, p. 1.

A few books by George Sand
with date of publication:

1832	Indiana - La Marquise - Valentine
1833	Leila - Metella - Le Secretaire intime
1834	Leone Leoni - Andre - Lettres d'unvoyageur -
	Mattea - Jacques
1835	Lettres d'un voyageur
1836	Simon
1837	Mauprat - Les Maitres Mosaistes -
	La Ma Derniere Aldini L'Unscoque
1838	Les Sept cordes de lay lyre - Spiridion
1839	Gabriel *(play)* - Cosima
1840	Le Compagnon du tour de France
1841	Horace
1842	Consuelo
1843	La Comtesse de Rudolstadt
1844	Jeanne - Le Meunier d'angibault
1845	Le Peche de Monsieur Antoine - La Mare du diable
1846	Lucrezia Floriani
1847	Francois le Champi
1848	Histoire de man vie
1851	Claude - Le Mariage de Victorine *(plays)*
1853	Les Maitres sonneus
1854	Maitre Favilla
1856	La Daniella
1857	Les Beau - Messieurs de Bois - Core
1858	L'Homme de neige - Elle et Lui
1860	Le Marquis de Villemer - Valvedre
1862	Mademoiselle La Quintinie
1865	Monsieur Sylvestre
1867	Mademoiselle Marquem
1869	Pierre qui roule
1870	Malgretout - Cesarine Dietrich
1871	Journal d'un voyageur pendant la guerre
1872	Contes d'uine grand-mere - Flamarance

Her numerous novels are traditionally divided into four types:

1) **Idealistic, lyrical, romantic;** defending rights of women,
   e.g. Indiana, Valentine (1832), and Leila (1833).
2) **Mystico-socialistic;** favored mingling of socio-economic classes
   through love and intermarriage (1840s).
3) **Simple country themes** (following her disappointment at the failure
   of the Revolution of 1848).
4) **Modern sentimental love stories** (1860s).

HARRIET ROSS TUBMAN

1820 ? - 1913

DRAMATIC READING

by

MEG BOWMAN

"Freedom ain't bought with dust."

HARRIET ROSS TUBMAN

The Granger Collection

Harriet Tubman, an escaped slave, made 19 perilous journeys back into the South to bring more than 300 slaves north to freedom. During the Civil War, she served the Union as a spy behind Confederate lines.

Harriet Ross Tubman

Harriet Ross was born around the same time as Susan B. Anthony (1820) and she died in 1913. Anthony died in 1906.

If I had the power, statues of both of these women would stand in every city in the USA. Yes, I would replace all statues of generals on horseback *(statues that glorify war)* with statues of my heroines, including Harriet Tubman, who dedicated her life to freedom.

Born into a loving family, but mistreated by slave owners, Harriet determined that she had a right to freedom or death, and if she couldn't have one, she would have the other. She escaped from a Maryland plantation around the age of 29, but she couldn't rest knowing that her family and others suffered under slavery. Facing the danger of being shot and the risk of being returned to slave status, Harriet made 19 trips back South and led over 300 people North, all the way to Canada after passage of the 1850 Fugitive Slave Act under which **no** African American was safe.

Harriet Tubman was never caught, despite the handicaps of being illiterate, having a pronounced scar on her forehead, suffering narcolepsy, and slave owners offering a reward of $40,000* for her capture, dead or alive.

* *In 1990s dollars, almost $700,000.*

After being hit on the forehead with a piece of metal by an overseer, she suffered narcolepsy and never knew when sleeping spells would occur. She used disguises and subterfuge to escape capture, such as pretending to read when on a train headed South. She was called the "Moses" of her people and she never lost a "passenger" on the Underground Railroad.

During the Civil War (1861-65), Harriet Ross Tubman was a nurse, a spy, a scout and a leader of successful military expeditions. After the Civil War, always poor, she sold chickens and vegetables door-to-door in order to earn money to support her *Home for Old Coloured Folks* in Auburn, New York.

In 1903 she turned her home and 25 acres of land over to the African Methodist Episcopal Zion Church of Auburn, to be used as a home for the sick, the poor, the homeless, though she continued to live there herself. She wanted it called the John Brown Home. To her dismay, the church began to charge an admittance fee.

Always compassionate, Harriet said: *"When I give the Home over to Zion Church, what do you suppose they did? Why, they made a rule that nobody should come in without a hundred dollars. Now I wanted to make a rule that nobody could come in unless they had no money. What's the good of a Home if a person who wants to get in has to have money?" (See Ann Petry Harriet Tubman, pp. 219-220.)*

HARRIET ROSS TUBMAN

1820? - 1913

Dramatic Reading

by

Meg Bowman

"Freedom ain't bought with dust."

This short Dramatic Reading takes place in 1901 in Auburn, New York. It is a fictional interview of Harriet Ross Tubman by a fictional reporter when she is about 80 years old. However, the events described are based on historical records.

HARRIET ROSS TUBMAN

From the Blockson Afro-American collection.

HARRIET ROSS TUBMAN

CAST:

Harriet Ross Tubman .... Age: about 81

Reporter .... Young; can be male or female

Voice Off/ or On Stage........... Male or Female

SETTING:

Auburn, New York in the year 1901.
Early Fall.
Apples are being harvested.

Porch of Harriet Tubman's
Home for Old Coloured Folks.

<u>PROPS</u>:

Two chairs.

One table upon which there is a basket of apples.

Harriet Tubman is dressed in a simple, long work dress.

Reporter is dressed in a turn-of-the-19th-century style, and has a note pad and a pencil.

NOTE:
This dramatic readings takes about 20 minutes. There is no memorizing. Caution readers to speak loudly and clearly and to look up at one another rather than always looking down at their script.

182

HARRIET ROSS TUBMAN:
DRAMATIC READING

VOICE OFF/or ON STAGE:

The year is 1901.

We are at the "Home For Old Coloured Folks"*
in Auburn, New York.

This home was founded by Harriet Tubman after
the Civil War and has been supported by her ever
since.

Harriet Ross Tubman was an escaped slave who
returned to the South at least 19 times and
escorted over 300 slaves to Freedomland.

Illiterate, identifiable by a deep scar on her forehead, coping with narcolepsy**, there was a price
of $40,000. on her head, dead or alive.

That's about $700,000 today.

* *Home For The Aged and Indigent.*
  When she purchased 25 adjacent acres,
  it became the Harriet Tubman Home.

** *A condition characterized by brief attacks*
   of sleep which can last from a few moments
   to a few hours.

Harriet Ross Tubman was never caught and she never lost a "passenger" on the Underground Railroad.

During the Civil War, Harriet Ross Tubman was a nurse, a spy, a scout for the Union Army, and she is the only known woman to design, organize and lead military campaigns.

A true heroine, in every aspect of the word.

TUBMAN: (SITTING BY TABLE,
                  SORTING APPLES)

             (singing)

             "Go down, Moses,
             Way down in Egypt lan'...
             hmmm... hmmm...
             Tell o' Pharaoh...
             Let my people go..."

REPORTER: (ENTERING)

Mrs. Tubman?

I'm a reporter from the Times.
Heard you received an invitation
to visit Queen Victoria in England.

TUBMAN: Sho' did.

REPORTER: Are you planning to go?

TUBMAN: *(Sho')* wish I had de money...
be a real honor.

But I ain't...

REPORTER: Did the Queen really send you some gifts?

TUBMAN: Sho' did.
Sent a silk shawl an' a real purty
necklace... an' a medal and a letter
of congratulations... for de things
I do *(a)* long time ago.

Sit down; rest yo'self a spell.

REPORTER: (SITTING)

Mrs. Tubman, how old are you now?

TUBMAN: (LOOKING OVER APPLES)

Don't rightly know.
Born 'bout 1820, I reckon.

REPORTER: Well, it's 1901 now, so that makes you
about 80 or 81 years old.
How are you feeling?

TUBMAN: Fit.
No complaints.
Keeps busy takin' care of de old folks.

REPORTER: (LOOKING AT NOTES)

Home For Old Coloured Folks, the Aged
and the Indigent.

How is that supported?
Where do you get the money?

TUBMAN: Sells chickens door-to-door....
vegetables, an' now dese heah apples.
(NODS HEAD AFFIRMATIVELY)

Gits a little pension...   an' a little
money from de book Sarah Bradford
write ' bout me.

REPORTER: (LOOKING AT NOTES)

"Scenes in the Life of Harriet Tubman,"
published in 1869.*

TUBMAN: (NODDING IN AGREEMENT)

Tells 'bout my childhood an' de
Underground Railroad... de War, too.

REPORTER: Let's see, you were born on a
plantation in Maryland — about 1820.

TUBMAN: Ben Ross was my pappy, an' my
mammy was Ol' Rit. *(She)* had de same
name as me, Harriet...
Called her Rit.
They was fine people. Yes, suh, good folks.

REPORTER: You had several brothers and sisters.

TUBMAN: Eleven.

Brought most of 'em out of slavery...
dose not sold 'down de river'.

* *Sarah H. Bradford also wrote* <u>Harriet, The Moses of Her People</u>, *1886.*

(SHAKES HEAD SADLY)

Slavery... terrible... terrible...

Ain't right, folks makin' slaves of other
folks.   Jus' ain't right!

REPORTER: You were abused as a child?

TUBMAN: Worked to de bone, Chile!
I was strong den.

I ain't big, but I'se strong.

Had me totin' water to de field hands, den
takin' care of babies,   den choppin'   down
trees and workin' de fields...

Mastah indenture me out...
Yes, suh, Mastah make a heap 'a money....
Had me workin' for other folks.

Ran way once, hid in de pig sty...fightin'
dos little piglets for potato peelin's....

REPORTER: What happened?

TUBMAN: Sent back to de mastah...
he a mean man.

188

Mastah, he have dese contests....make me
pull a barge of stones' long de river bank...
hard, hard work... jus' so de mastah have
a contest... an' all dese men folk, dey be
bettin' on how far I pull dose rocks....

REPORTER: Are you saying they made sport of you?

TUBMAN: (NODDING IN AGREEMENT)

          Not right, no suh, not right.

REPORTER: That scar on your forehead?

TUBMAN: Got t'wix dis overseer an' a slave...
          ' bout to run away.

          Overseer, he throw dis iron, hit me right
          here...

          (POINTS TO LEFT TEMPLE)

          Ever'body thought, **fo' sho'**, I die...
          Mammy Rit, she nurse me, many a day...

          (LAUGHS)
          You can see I lives.... but de spells,
          jus' go to sleep, most anywhere, anytime....
          called narco-lep-sy.

REPORTER: Tell me about your escape from
this Maryland plantation.

TUBMAN: Well, I had married up wid John
Tubman.

I tell John, "Dere's two things I got a right
to—freedom or death.
If I can't have one, I **will** have de other."

John, he free.
Wouldn't go wid me.
I'se 'bout 30 years old den, an' took off....
'cross de Choptank River. Cold.

Sleep durin' de day, travel by night.
Keep lookin' for dat North Star.

Keep feelin' de moss on de trees,
 goin' North.
When I gits to Pennsylvania,
I was in Freedomlan'....

I looked at my hands to see if I was de
same person. There was such a glory
 over ever'thing.
De sun came shining like gold
through the trees, an' I felt like I was
in Heaven.
I was **free**!

REPORTER: Where did you go?

TUBMAN: Philadelphia.
I was a stranger in a strange land.

Worked wid de abolitionists. Radicals.
Wanted to end slavery.

(I) scrubbed floors, washed dishes, cooked,
cleaned...   Saved dat money.

(You) see, I couldn't rest.
I'd heard de moans of my people.
My kinfolk, still slaves.

No, suh, I couldn't rest.
I had to do somethin'.

REPORTER: I understand that you made at least 19 trips
back South and rescued over 300 people.

TUBMAN: Sho' did. Sho'ly did do dat.

After dat Fugitive Slave Law pass in '50,
took 'em all de way to Canada.

No coloured safe den... No-suh-re...
(We had to) be under de paw of de **British**
Lion.

191

REPORTER: Did you take your parents all the
way to Canada?

TUBMAN: Did, indeed, back in 18 and 57.

Ol' Rit wouldn't go widout her feather tick
— an' her chickens.

Kinda "borrowed" dis ol' rickety carriage
an' dis ol' horse — older dan Mathusula...

(LAUGHS)

Put in dat mattress, put in dat chicken coop,
an' den stole off into de night.
Took many weeks, but we make it —all de
way to St. Catharines, Canada.

REPORTER: I've read that slaveowners offered
a reward of $40,000. for your capture —
dead or alive.
That's **a lot** of money! *

TUBMAN: *(Dey)* wanted me bad, but I fool 'em.

See, I know de back roads, de hidin' places,
de good places to stay on de Underground
Railroad....

* *About $700,000 in 1990s money.*

192

REPORTER: Just what was this Underground Railroad?

TUBMAN: When I first hear 'bout it, I think it a real train... under de ground.

(LAUGHS)

But it be coloured folks an' white folks *(who)* give us food an' shelter.

REPORTER: How did it work?

TUBMAN: See, I go by de slave shanties an' sing de song--

(SINGS)

"Steal away, steal away....
Steal away to Jesus...."

Dat be de signal an' dose ready to run, dey join me.
We hide in de potato cellars, in de attics, in false bottoms on de wagons. Once, we crawl in, dey put some planks over us, and we git covered wid bricks... jus' to cross dis bridge 'cause it be guarded.... but we git to Wilmington, to Thomas Garrett's house. *(Did)* you know Thomas Garrett?

THOMAS GARRETT

Prominent Quaker of Wilmington, Delaware, businessman, and active in the Underground Railroad. (From the Blockson Afro-American collection.)

WILLIAM STILL

*Agent for the Philadelphia Underground Railroad.
(From Blockson Afro-American collection.)*

194

REPORTER: No... Businessman....? Died about 30
years ago....? Owned a shoe store?

TUBMAN: He **sell** shoes to de white folks, but he **give**
shoes to God's poor.
Dat's what he call us, God's poor.

Had a false wall in de store, we hide
behind it. Always have milk and biscuits
an' free shoes for ever'body.

REPORTER: How did you raise funds
to finance your trips South?

TUBMAN: De Vigilance Committee —William Still —
in Philadelphia — he a coloured man.

Dey give me money.
Den, I make speeches at de Anti-Slavery
an' at de Woman's Suffrage meetin's....
Once, I go to dis man's office an' tell de
man I needs twenty dollahs.

He say, " Go away! Dere's no money
for you, Harriet. "

I say, "No, I just sits here'til I gits de
money."

Sat dere all day.

195

Go to sleep, sittin' dere on de floor.

While I'se sleepin', folks must have
passed by 'cause when I wakes up,
dere's $60. in my lap!

(LAUGHS)

REPORTER: (TO AUDIENCE)

This surely must be one of the first sit-ins.

(TO HARRIET)

Did you have any close calls —
almost captured?

TUBMAN: Oh, many, many...
One time, on de train.... gwine South.

See, dose slavecatchers don't think
I ever be gwine South.

An' when dey look at me, I pick up a book
an' act like I'm readin'....

Dey say, "Dat can't be de one called Moses,
cause she can't read!"

(LAUGHS)

196

REPORTER: I have read that you were a master at
disguises.... even dressed in men's
clothes, and sometimes you pretended
to be much older than you were.

TUBMAN: Sho' did.
Act like an ol' granny.

Onct, I was in Bucktown down
in Mar'land an' I see my ol' mastah....
he be on a horse.
Real quick, I buy two chickens, tie 'em
'round my neck and pretend to be **real** old.

When he ride by, I let dose chickens go...
dey flutter, cause a commotion, an' Mastah
yell, "Go it, Granny! I bet on de chickens!"

Fooled dat man....

(CHUCKLES)

Sho' did....

REPORTER: And you were called Moses, because
you led people out of slavery.

It is said that of the 300 or so people you
led out of slavery, not one turned back.

TUBMAN: Never lost a passenger.

Some found de goin' kinda hard... *(they)* wanted to go back, but I couldn't *(al)* low dat.

No, suh!

Dey git whupped, have to tell de mastah de hidin' places an' de names of de good people dat help us....

I jus' aim my rifle at dere head an' I say, "Dead mens tell no tales. You go on wid us or you die!"

REPORTER: (LOOKING AT NOTES)

Let's see, you were about 29 or 30 when you escaped.

Why was it that your husband didn't go with you?

TUBMAN: John, he be free.

He like Mar'land, but I'se 'fraid I be sold down de river—dat's de Mississippi River — to de delta country.

I come back for John, but he had hisself
 a new wife....

So I jus' keep takin' dose runaways up
to Freedomlan'.

REPORTER: And you supported John Brown?

TUBMAN: Sho' did!
He a **good** man.

A good white man.... saw de evil of slavery.

Wanted to free **all** de slaves.
Yes-suh, he be my friend.

Fact is, I be dere with ol' John Brown on dat
Harper's Ferry raid, wid his sons, but I was
sick, and den it was too late.

Yes suh, dey hung Cap'n Brown,
but his soul go marchin' on.

REPORTER: He called you **General** Tubman,
and you **did** lead military expeditions
during the Civil War.

TUBMAN: Planned, organized, led dose raids...
wid Colonel Montgomery.

John Brown, a Kansas abolitionist, recruited a band of 17 white men and five black men in 1859 and led them in a desperate raid against the federal arnsenal at Harper's Ferry, Virginia, to capture arms for a slave revolt. All but one of the men were killed, wounded or captured. Brown and two others were later tried and hanged.

JOHN BROWN

(The Granger Collection)

He fought wid John Brown in Kansas...

He know de guerrilla tactics.

We go into South Carolina... bring out de contraband.

First, de slaves, de contraband, 'fraid of us, but after Lincoln sign dat 'Mancipation Proclamation, an' dey learn we was Lincoln's army *(there)* to set 'em free, den dey come by de hun'reds.... an' de hun'reds... **oo-eee**, dat was a sight to behold!

REPORTER: And you were a spy?

TUBMAN: For de Union.

REPORTER: And a nurse....

TUBMAN: Terrible, terrible...
War be blood an' pain, an' flies, an' death.

I bake pies an' gingerbread, an' make root beer *(in order to)* raise de money to buy de bandages.

My daddy, Ol' Ben, he taught me
how to make medicines... wid roots,
berries, flowers an' such.

I wash de wounds, tend to de sick....

REPORTER: And you organized hospitals.

TUBMAN: (NODDING HEAD IN AGREEMENT)

Got de nurses organized....
dey my friends.

REPORTER: And you were never paid.

TUBMAN: Got a gover'ment pass for de train,
but after de war, I gits on dis train,
gwine back to New York.... an' de
conductor say,"What you doin' wid
a gover'ment pass?
You ain't no soldier!"
Dey gang up on me an' throw me
in de baggage car.

REPORTER: Did the federal government ever
give you a pension?

TUBMAN: Try an' try to git dat pension.

            Generals, ever'body write to
            de gover'ment.... but, no help.

            Finally, in 18 and 69, I decide
            to marry up wid Nelson an'
            when he die in '88....

            Nelson, he a veteran....
            had de tuberculosis....

            Den I gits $8. a month.

            Den, in '97, Pres'dent Pierce,
            he sign de bill...
            so now, I gits $20. a month.*

REPORTER: You and Nelson fixed up this house
            to take in old coloured folks....

TUBMAN: Yes-suh, after de war, lots of folks
            needin' a home....
            No money. We poor, but we take
            good care of de old folks.

*In the Spring of 1869, Harriet married a veteran Nelson Davis
who, although more than 20 years younger than she, was unable to
contribute to the support of the household. He died October 14, 1888
and it was not until 1899 that Harriet was awarded a pension of $20. a
month as the widow of Nelson Davis.*

Wid de pension, an' me goin' door-to-door
sellin' chickens an' dese apples --
(HOLDS UP AN APPLE)
Well, I keeps de wolf from de door.

REPORTER: I see you're sorting apples.

TUBMAN: You like apples?

REPORTER: Sure do.

TUBMAN: You ever plant an apple tree?

REPORTER: No, can't say that I have.

TUBMAN: *(No, but)* somebody else plant 'em.

See, when I was young... like you....
I likes apples, too.

But I was a slave and it was
forbidden to eat the fruit on the trees.

An' I say, ' Someday I plant apple
trees so dere be apples for de young
folks comin' after....'

An', I guess I did.

(GIVES AN APPLE TO THE REPORTER)

Yes-suh, I surely did!

REPORTER: (STANDING)

Thank you.
Mrs. Tubman, you are, indeed,
a remarkable woman.
A **heroine**, in every sense
of the word.

TUBMAN: (STANDING)

An' I thanks all dese folks
(INDICATING AUDIENCE)

come to meet Moses an' keep freedom on
dere mind.

(TO AUDIENCE)

Now, ol' Moses, she work for Freedom....
an' Freedom ain't bought wid dust, no suh.
Freedom be hard work.

Freedom be learnin' history an' 'bout
de gover'ment.

Freedom be votin' and makin' de laws.

Freedom be de pursuit of happiness
and gwine where you wants to go.

So, you-all jus' keep on keepin' on,
cuzz Freedom ain't bought wid dust.
No -suh, Freedom ain't bought wid dust.

(REPORTER AND TUBMAN
 IN FREEZE POSITION)

###

After applause, the following afterthought is optional:
VOICE OFF/ or ON STAGE:

Harriet Ross Tubman was a heroine in every sense of the word. Meg Bowman, the author, says that if she had the power, there would be a statue of Harriet Tubman in every city in the United States.

Here is a description of a 'heroine' written by Andrea Fleck Clardy that seems to fit the word:

"We grow in spirals, circling the past and moving toward the possible, nurtured by ideas and insights as much as by healthy breakfasts. We grow because someone we meet in a book or on the job or in a chance encounter pushes us past our easy certainties and expands the scope of our vision.

Our heroines broaden the base of our becoming, spark our imagination and encourage our commitment to do more than the expected, to be all that we can dream. We need to celebrate those whose names we have known since childhood. We need to discover those who have been hidden from history and those whose good work is now in progress. For our heroines inspire us to continue growing, not in size but in stature, not in one direction but in many dimensions."*

Harriet Ross Tubman, you inspire us to be all that we can dream. You inspire us to continue growing. **You are our heroine.**

Harriet Ross Tubman and Reporter, please take a bow. We applaud you!

* Andrea Fleck Clardy, *"Heroines '84"*
Crossing Press, Trumansburg, NY 14886.

207

Frederick Douglass, a fugitive slave and
skilled abolitionist orator.
(J.B. Lieb Photo Co.)

FREDERICK DOUGLASS ON HARRIET TUBMAN

"Most that I have done and suffered in the service of our cause has been in public, and I have received much encouragement at every step of the way. You on the other hand have labored in a private way. I have wrought in the day — you in the night. I have had the applause of the crowd and the satisfaction that comes of being approved by the multitude, while the most that you have done has been witnessed by a few trembling, scared and foot-sore bondsmen and women, whom you have led out of the house of bondage whose heartfelt 'God Bless you' has been your only reward. The midnight sky and the silent stars have been the witnesses of your devotion to freedom and of your heroism. Excepting John Brown — of sacred memory — I know of no one who has willingly encountered more perils and hardships to serve our enslaved people than you have. Much that you have done would seem improbable to those who do not know you as I know you."

— Frederick Douglass

Death of a Heroine

In March, 1913, at age 93, Harriet Tubman contracted pneumonia. Just before her death *(3/10/1913)* she conducted her own farewell service, leading those at her bedside in the singing of old spirituals. The local newspaper described her deathbed scene as thrilling a chapter in her life as any of the previous acts during the heroic drama of her life. Her death was national news and, although awarded very late, honors were finally bestowed upon her. In June 1914 flags were flown at half-mast as Auburn dedicated a bronze tablet to their great townswoman. Thousands heard Booker T. Washington and others pay homage to Harriet Ross Tubman and her struggle for freedom.

The bronze plaque which was placed at the front entrance of the County Court House reads:

> IN MEMORY OF HARRIET TUBMAN.
> BORN A SLAVE IN MARYLAND ABOUT 1821.
> DIED IN AUBURN, N.Y., MARCH 10th, 1913.
> CALLED THE MOSES OF HER PEOPLE, WITH RARE
> COURAGE SHE LED OVER THREE HUNDRED
> NEGROES UP FROM SLAVERY TO FREEDOM,
> AND DURING THE CIVIL WAR,
> RENDERED INVALUABLE SERVICE
> AS NURSE AND SPY.
> WITH IMPLICIT TRUST IN GOD
> SHE BRAVED EVERY DANGER AND
> OVERCAME EVERY OBSTACLE, WITHAL
> SHE POSSESSED EXTRAORDINARY
> FORESIGHT AND JUDGMENT SO THAT
> SHE TRUTHFULLY SAID
> "ON MY UNDERGROUND RAILROAD
> I NEBBER RUN MY TRAIN OFF DE TRACK
> AN' I NEBBER LOS' A PASSENGER."
> THIS TABLE IS ERECTED
>
> BY THE CITIZENS OF AUBURN.

BIBLIOGRAPHY *(partial)*

Bradford, Sarah Hopkins, *Scenes in the Life of Harriet Tubman* (Books for Libraries Press, 1971 reprint of 1869 edition).

Buckmaster, Henrietta *(pseud)*, *Women Who Shaped History* (Collier Books, 1966).

Conrad, Earl, *Harriet Tubman: Negro Soldier and Abolitionist* (International Publishers, 1942).

Epstein, Sam and Beryl, *Harriet Tubman: Guide To Freedom* (Garrard, 1968).

Heidish, Marcy, *A Woman Called Moses: A novel based on the life of Harriet Tubman* (Houghton Mifflin, 1976).

Lawrence, Jacob, *Harriet and the Promised Land* (Windmill Books, 1968).

McGovern, Ann, *Runaway Slave; the Story of Harriet Tubman* (Four Winds Press, 1965).

Metcalf, George R., *Black Profiles* (McGraw Hill, 1968).

Petry, Ann, *Harriet Tubman: Conductor on the Underground Railroad* (Thomas Y Crowell/Archway Paperback, 1955; 1971).

Sillen, Samuel, *Women Against Slavery* (Masses and Mainstream, 1955, pp. 47-53).

Sterling, Dorothy, *Freedom Train: The Story of Harriet Tubman* (Doubleday/Scholastic Books, 1954).

Sterling, Philip, *Four Took Freedom; the Lives of Harriet Tubman, Frederick Douglass, Robert Smalls, and Blanche K. Bruce* (Doubleday, 1967).

FEELINGS

DRAMATIC READING
IN
FIVE SCENES

by
Meg Bowman

(Based on a story by Rod Walter)

213

FEELINGS

This Dramatic Reading illustrates one man's inability to get in touch with his feelings.

It requires three (3) female readers and three (3) male readers.

There are only a few suggested props and no memorizing.

Caution readers to speak loudly and clearly.

SETTING: Working-class kitchen, Salinas Valley,
           California.
           It is early evening. The family has just
           returned from a Labor Day picnic and
           Babs is ironing her waitress uniform for
           work tomorrow.

CAST: Babs: In her early 40s, she works as a
           full-time waitress at Denny's—the one
           out on the highway. She is expected to
           do all the housework.

           Fred: In his mid-40s, he is a fork-lift
           operator at a canning plant. His job
           makes him feel powerful. He spends his
           evenings drinking beer, watching sports
           on TV, and channel surfing.

           Gloria: Fred and Bab's daughter. At
           age 16, she hangs out at the Mall and
           does not take her school work seriously.

           Michael: A well-mannered young man
           about to graduate from high school; he
           works part-time at a local gas station.

           Psychologist: Career woman who
           works with inmates at a state prison.

           Psychologist's husband: He is support-
           ive of his wife's concerns for inmates.

SUGGESTED PROPS: Ironing board
(none are essential)   Iron
    Plastic water bottle
    Two chairs
    Remote control
    (televison)
    Empty beer can
    Rifle

*Babs is ironing, Gloria is standing in the doorway.
Fred can be seen off-stage as if in the living room,
sitting in a chair, watching TV and drinking a can of
beer. He has a television remote control in his hand.*

BABS: *(ironing)* Ahhh, I need a cool shower....
          Maybe a bubble bath....

        (sighs)   I just wish Fred or Gloria
        would help me once in awhile....
        (wipes perspiration from her face)

        That Labor Day picnic wore me out.
        Ahhhh....
        So **bleepin'** hot!

GLORIA: *(standing by door)*
         Mother, I need to talk to you.

BABS: Oh, yeah?   What about?
        Look, Gloria, I got ironin' to do.

GLORIA: I think I've got a problem.

BABS: So? What else is new?

GLORIA: Moh-ther! Please!

BABS: Okay, okay. If it isn't one **bleepin'** thing,
           it's another.
           Wait 'til I finish this ironin'.

GLORIA: No, Mom, I need to talk right now.
           It's **serious**!
           Honest.

BABS: *(sighs)* Oh, **bleep!**
           Okay, what kind of serious?
           Another zit on your face?

GLORIA: Serious, serious, Mother.

           (lowers her voice)

           And don't tell Daddy.

           It's just between you and me.
           Okay? Okay????

BABS: Yeah, yeah, okay.
Hand me that jug of water.

*(Gloria hands Babs a plastic bottle
of water, and Babs puts water
into the iron.)*

So, Gloria, what's so serious?

Go ahead, talk.

GLORIA: *(whispers)* I think, well, I guess,
maybe....
I think I'm pregnant.

BABS: Whaaat?! *(knocks iron to floor)*

FRED: *(calls out)* Ev'rything okay in there?

BABS: *(shouts)* Yeh, Fred, no problem.
I just dropped the iron, that's all.

FRED: Well, for **Bleep's** sake, be careful.
Those things cost me money!

BABS: *(to Gloria)*
Yeh, sure....**my** tips paid
for **this** iron.

(picks up iron)

219

Now, whaddaya mean, you **think**,
maybe, perhaps you're pregnant?
How d'you know?

GLORIA: Well, I.... I've missed two periods and
I feel kinda, well... funny-like....

BABS: *(angry)* Who the **bleep** was it?
When did it happen?

GLORIA: Oh, Mother, don't be mad.
Please, Mom, don't be mad.

It was Michael, Michael Sanders, at that
beach party the church had last June.
Remember?

Michael doesn't know.
I haven't told **anyone**....
and I haven't seen Michael since the
beach party....
honest, haven't seen him
all summer.

*(embarassed and biting her lip,
she stares at the floor)*

BABS: I wondered 'bout that beach party.
(Scowls)

220

Didn't like the sound of it.
I shouldn't have let you go.

But it was the church an' all.
I didn't figure anything could
happen there.

(angry) **Bleep** it anyway!

(aside to audience)

Dammit, what'll people think?
I brung Gloria up not to bleep around.
She's a good girl, not like I was
at her age.

If she has a kid everybody will know it.

And they'll know she's been
bleepin' around.
Sure don't want people talking about me
like I ain't been a good mother.

Abortion? No.
Ev'rybody'll find out about that, too.

Besides, what'll Brother Bob, the pastor,
say?

He's down there in front of the Family Planning Clinic every week with those signs and his bullhorn protestin' abortions goin' on.

He'd kick us out of the church for sure.

(gets an idea)

Wait a minute!
Brother Bob said that abortion was okay if the girl was raped. Aha!

(to Gloria)

Gloria! You **didn't** wanna do it, did you?

GLORIA: Huh? Wud-do-ya-mean, Mom*?*
            (near tears)

BABS: I mean, it was all **his** fault, right?

GLORIA: All **his** fault? Huh? You look so mad....
            He said he loved me and I told him....

BABS: *(interrupts)* You **didn't** wanna do it,
did you?

He **forced** himself on you, didn't he?

GLORIA: No.

*(confused and doesn't know if that's
the right answer)*

What should I say, Mom? Huh?
You look so mad....

BABS: No?! You mean you **let him?**

(raises her hand as if to slap Gloria)

You slut!
I told you about boys and never
to let 'em....

GLORIA: *(steps back frightened and cowers
against the wall)*

I mean, **yes**, Mother.

*(Fred quietly gets out of the chair and,
holding an empty beer can, walks
to the doorway: neither Babs nor
Gloria see him standing at the door)*

BABS: Yes? You mean you **wanted** him
to do it?
Come here, you **bleepin'** little whore!

GLORIA: No, no.... I mean, I **didn't** want him
to do it.

Yes, he **raped** me....
Michael raped me....

BABS: *(smiling)*
You know what that means, don't you?

You're gonna hafta get rid of it.
You're gonna hafta get an abortion.

(sees Fred at the door)

Oh, no! You didn't **hear** that, did you?

FRED: I sure as **bleep** did. *(angry)*
What Michael was it, the one at the gas
station?

(not getting an answer, he bellows)

Where the **bleep's** my keys?
I'll get that little **bleep!**
No pimply faced **bleep** is gonna **bleep**
<u>my</u> daughter and get away with it.

224

(throws his empty beer can on the floor,
grabs car keys and stomps off stage)

BABS: No, Fred. Don't.... don't....

<u>SCENE TWO</u>

(Fred sits in a make-believe pick-up truck.
There is a rifle on the seat beside him.)

MICHAEL: Hi, Mr. Farrell. How are you?
               Want some gas?

FRED: Yeh. Gimme five gallons of regular.

MICHAEL: Want your oil checked?

FRED: No, uh, just get the windshield.

MICHAEL: *(pretends to insert the nozzle into the opening on the side of Fred's pick-up, and then returns to "wash" the windshield)*

How's Gloria these days? Haven't seen her in a long time.

FRED: I'll bet you haven't, you little **bleep!**

Bleep her and forget her, right?

MICHAEL: Huh? *(doesn't understand)*

Tell her 'hello' for me, will you? Last time I saw her.... *(looks up)*

FRED: *(pointing rifle directly at Michael's head)*

Rape my daughter, eh?

*(pumps two bullets directly into Michael's head **"Bang! Bang!"** Michael collapses and falls to the floor)*

Bleep it! Now I'll hafta clean the windshield again.

*(gets out of pick-up and walks to
make-believe phone and dials)*

Police? Hello, police station?
I just killed the **bleep** who raped
my daughter.

You better come and get me.
I've got a gun.

*(Gloria and Babs run on-stage as if they
have just driven up and when they see
Michael's body, both women scream)*

BABS: Gloria, **don't** look. Don't look, Gloria!

GLORIA: *(goes to Fred)*   Oh, poor Daddy.
               Poor, poor Daddy....

BABS: Poor Daddy, hell! He's going to jail.
               We can't get along on just my job.
               Now **what the bleep** am I gonna do?
               Fred, how could you?!

FRED: Okay, Babs, so I killed the little **bleep**.
               No one rapes **my** daughter and gets
               away with it.

227

SCENE THREE

*(In prison. Psychologist is talking to Fred.
They are both seated.)*

FRED: You shrinks just don't understand.
Right away, I knew I had to kill the
bleep who done it.

PSYCHOLOGIST: Yes, Fred. But how did you **feel**
about it?

FRED: *(confused)* Huh?
I thought I just told you....

PSYCHOLOGIST: You told me what you thought
you must do to avenge your
daughter's disgrace, but what
were you **feeling**?

FRED: Feeling?

PSYCHOLOGIST: Yes.

FRED: Well, uh, first off, I wondered where
             to put my, uh, empty beer can, and
             then when I got my keys,
             I wondered if the pick-up would
             start okay.
             I've been havin' a little trouble
             with it.

PSYCHOLOGIST: Yes, I understand.
               I guess what I'm probing
               for is whether you remember
               experiencing any particular
               feelings.

               *(Fred shakes his head
               and scowls)*

               You do know what a feeling is,
               don't you, Mr. Farrell?

FRED: Well, uh, sure, I guess....
             A feeling is, uh, you know, like,
             somethin' you feel.

PSYCHOLOGIST: That's right.
What you've told me so far is
what you thought, and what
you did, but **not** what you felt.

FRED: *(trying to make sense of what the*
psychologist is saying)

Feeling? Hmmmm....
Well, I just felt that I had to get in my
truck and go down to the gas station
and, you know....
Didn't I already say that?

PSYCHOLOGIST: Ah, now we're getting
somewhere.

FRED: *(smiling)*

I said the right thing?

PSYCHOLOGIST: Well, no.
Not really.
Actually, you said
the 'wrong' thing.
You said that you felt **that**....

FRED: *(shrugging his shoulders)*

            So? What's wrong with **that**?

PSYCHOLOGIST: You weren't expressing
                  a **feeling**, Fred.

            You were still saying what it was
            you decided to do.
            If you follow the words <u>felt</u> or
            <u>feeling</u> with the word **that** —
            you aren't expressing a feeling,
            you are saying what you want
            to do, or what you **did**.

            Do you know what you would say
            to **tell me** what your feelings
            were?

FRED: *(to audience)*

            These head-shrinkers are crazy!

            (to psychologist)

            No, what?

PSYCHOLOGIST: You would say something like,
                'I felt confused' or 'I felt angry'.
                Did you feel angry, Fred?

FRED: *(still puzzled)*

           Angry? Angry, like when I push
           Babs around and give her 'what for'
           — and she deserves it, too?

           She **bleepin'** well knows how I feel.
           So why do I hafta say what I feel?
           Babs can tell.... Can't you tell?

PSYCHOLOGIST: Yes, Fred, I can tell.

FRED: So?

PSYCHOLOGIST: So, if you don't express your
                feelings in words, Fred, they boil
                and bubble around inside of you
                and give you problems—
                emotional and health problems—
                or they come out in actions.

                With you, your anger came out
                in action, a deadly action.
                You killed a young man.

232

                    Imagine the difference if you had
                    expressed your anger in words
                    instead.

FRED: *(he has no idea what she's talking
                    about)*

                    What?

PSYCHOLOGIST: You might have said to your wife,
                    'Babs, if what I have just heard
                    is true, I feel very, very angry.
                    I feel a sense of injustice, too.

                    It isn't right for a young man
                     to take advantage of a girl, if,
                     in fact, that is what happened.

                    I think Michael should be
                    punished for what he did
                    to Gloria,' and so on....

                    You see, Mr. Farrell, by verbaliz-
                    ing anger in words, the anger
                    subsides, uh, it goes down, and
                    you would feel less like driving
                    impulsively, you know, without
                    thinking, down to the gas station
                    and doing what you did.

You'd be better able to reason the problem through, perhaps think of other solutions.

Does that make sense?

FRED: *(mouth wide open. Then he gets up from his chair, and walks back and forth, shaking his head. He looks at the psychologist.)*

You oughta come to the plant

sometime... where I work, and try to explain to the guys down there that instead of blowin' that **bleeper's** brains out for what he did to my daughter, I said stuff like that. You oughta just try tellin' the guys that, and see what they think.... Yeah, see what they think....

SCENE FOUR

*(Psychologist and her husband are seated
in their home.)*

PSYCHOLOGIST: You know, honey, I feel discour-
aged sometimes...
 about my work.
It seems as if I just can't get
through to some of the prisoners,
particularily in regards to having
them identify and describe their
feelings.

HUSBAND: Yes, I know it's tough...
Men are carefully taught from a
very early age **not** to be in touch
with their feelings.

PSYCHOLOGIST: Men stuff their anger and then it
explodes.

I'm working with one prisoner, a
brilliant guy who was studying at
a prestigious university. His girl
friend dumped him, so he went to
her sorority house and shot her
to death.

235

Then, there's another prisoner
who **thought** that his daughter
had been raped, which wasn't
true at all....
but he killed this young man and,
well, I just don't know....

HUSBAND: Have you spoken to the Board about
the trouble you're having?

PSYCHOLOGIST: Yes, just yesterday.
They want me to keep on
They say that if more men would
express their feelings in words,
fewer of them would wind up in
prison for committing violent
crimes.

HUSBAND: Or get ulcers or heart attacks.
I wonder if people realize that most
prisoners are released back into
society?

Men are sentenced, they do their time,
and are back out on the street...
still filled with anger and feelings
they can't express....

SCENE FIVE

(Fred stands alone, center stage.)

FRED: Sure, I feel lonely....
I feel misunderstood.
I miss Babs and Gloria....
I miss my job and my pick-up...
I miss my rifle and my TV....
I miss my beer.
I miss being able to **bleep** Babs....
even punchin' her out to teach her
a lesson.

Well, at least **nobody** can say I ain't
a real man.
Nobody can say I didn't teach that
bleepin' gas jockey a thing or two.
Nobody's gonna rape my little girl
and get away with it.
No siree.

Damn! I feel good.
I feel super **bleepin' good!**

END

DISCUSSION:

Why did Fred kill Michael?
What is Fred's attitude toward Gloria?
 toward Babs?
Why does Fred think it's okay to batter Babs
(give her 'what for')?
What is Bab's attitude toward Fred?
Why does Babs want Gloria to accuse Michael
of rape?
Why does Fred feel 'super bleepin' good'?
Why are so many men unable to get in touch
with their feelings?
Why are our prisons filled with men who can
only express feelings of anger?
How can we socialize boys to be in touch with
their feelings?
to be truly complete human beings?

*Based on a story by Rod Walter, The Imaginary Village (Summer 1993);
revised into a dramatic reading by Meg Bowman (1995).*

FIVE WAYS TO KILL PEOPLE
(for two readers)

READER 1:   There are many cumbersome ways
to kill people.

READER 2:   You can force people to carry a plank
of wood to the top of a hill and then nail them to it.

READER 1:   To do this properly requires a crowd
wearing sandals, a cock that crows, a history of sadistic
dictatorships, and at least one man to hammer the nails.

READER 2:   Or, you can take a length of steel, shape
it into a sharp spear or lance and attempt to pierce
someone in a metal cage called armor.

READER 1:   But for this you need white horses,
English trees, men with bows and arrows, and at least
two flags.

READER 2:   And don't forget a prince and a castle
to hold your banquet in.

READER 1:   Dispensing with nobility, you may,
if the wind allows, blow poisoned gas at people.

READER 2:   But then you need a mile of mud sliced
through with ditches, not to mention black boots, bomb
craters, more mud, a plague of rats, a dozen patriotic
songs, and some round hats made of steel.

READER 1:   In an age of airplanes, you may fly miles
above your victims and dispose of them by pressing
a small switch.

READER 2:   All that is required is an imaginary line
to separate people, two systems of government, and
land that no one needs for several years.

READER 1:   There are, as we began, many cumbersome
ways to kill people.

READER 2:   Simpler, direct, and much more neat is
to continue polluting our planet.

READER 1:   Now, as we enter the twenty-first century,
we cut down the Rain Forests, spray pesticides, dump
toxic wastes, destroy the ozone layer, the Black Forest,
the coastlines, the oceans....

READER 2:   ...and leave us here, on our dying planet.

BOTH READERS: Yes, there are many, many ways
to kill people.

RESPONSIVE READINGS

TO ACKNOWLEDGE OUR ANCESTORS
(Responsive Reading)

To acknowledge our ancestors
is to be aware—

—THAT WE ARE THE HEIRS
OF ALL THE AGES.

To acknowledge our ancestors
is to honor those ancient women—

—WHO WORSHIPPED THE GODDESS,
THE WISE WOMEN,
THE HEALERS,
THE MIDWIVES.

To acknowledge our ancestors
is to feel empathy with—

—OUR **MOTHERS,**
GRANDMOTHERS,
GREAT-GRANDMOTHERS,
GREAT-GREAT GRANDMOTHERS.

Who moved from place-to-place,
continent-to-continent,
house-to-house.

SO THAT TODAY
WE FIND OURSELVES HERE
—AT THIS PLACE—
ACKNOWLEDGING OUR ANCESTORS.

Blessed Be our ancestors.

Meg Bowman

IT IS GOOD TO REMEMBER

Women, it is good to remember—

    —THAT WE ARE A LINK
    IN THE WEB OF LIFE.

Women, it is good to remember—

    —OUR ANCESTORS
    WHO HAVE GIVEN US LIFE.

Women, it is good to remember
    that we are **not**
    the first generation—

    —TO BE IN LOVE,
    TO RAISE CHILDREN,
    TO REBEL AGAINST INJUSTICES,
    TO CHALLENGE PATRIARCHY.

Women, it is good to remember
    that life is short
    and that we must—

ALL: CELEBRATE EACH DAY,
    TREASURE EACH MOMENT,
    LAUGH, LOVE, AND PLAY.

    BLESSED BE.   *Meg Bowman*

<u>Becoming</u>

Our Mother Earth, Who Abounds all Around us
Hallowed be Thy Name.
We know in our Hearts
Thy Power is Awesome, Thy beauty Serene.

Give us this day the will to Hope
And the Strength to Strive.
And give us Patience to Forgive,
As we would like to be Forgiven.
Lead us to overcome Temptation, Fear and Grief.

Clarify our Anger, that it may Direct our Efforts
Toward worthy Goals.
Wash clean our Spirits,
And renew our Senses, that we may Live
With Joy and Laughter.

For we are your Children
And we Celebrate the Life
You have Given Us,
Knowing that We are the Glory
And the Love and the Power
Forever and ever <u>Becoming</u>—

Blessed Be.

Meg Bowman

244

Benediction

May the truth that makes us free
And the hope that never dies,
And the love that casts out fear,

LEAD US FORWARD TOGETHER
UNTIL DAYLIGHT BREAKS
AND THE SHADOWS FLEE AWAY.

While we toil amidst things as they are,
May our vision of things yet to be

STRENGTHEN AND INSPIRE US.

May faithfulness to the good of each

BECOME THE UNFAILING VIRTUE
OF US ALL.

May our experience be enlightened
by understanding,

OUR LOVE ENNOBLED BY SERVICE,
AND OUR FAITH BE STRENGTHENED
BY KNOWLEDGE.

Blessed Be.

SOJOURNERS

Who are we, any of us, but strangers
  and sojourners forlornly wandering
  through the nighttime....

UNTIL WE DRAW TOGETHER
AND FIND THE MEANING
OF OUR LIVES
IN ONE ANOTHER

Dissolving our fears
  in each other's courage,
  making music together and lighting torches
  to guide us through the dark.

FOR 'LIFE IS RISK OR IT IS NOTHING AT ALL' *

It is good to be together again.
  Go in Peace.
  Make Peace.

BLESSED BE.

* Quote from Emma Goldman.